DIGITAL SOCIAL RELATIONSHIPS

Strategies and Techniques for Building a Strong and Lasting Online Presence

Disclaimer

This eBook is intended for informational functions simplest. Every effort has been made to ensure the eBook is as whole and correct as viable. However, there can be errors in typography or content material. Additionally, the records provided is correct most effective as of the guide date, and should be used as a manual in place of the definitive source.

The purpose of this eBook is to educate. The author and publisher make no guarantees about the completeness of the statistics and aren't accountable for any errors or omissions. Neither the author nor the writer shall have any liability or responsibility for any loss or harm, direct or indirect, caused or alleged to be resulting from this eBook.

This eBook gives facts for educational purposes best. It needs to not be relied upon alternatively for expert scientific advice, diagnosis, or treatment.

TABLE OF CONTENTS:

Part 1:

Foundations of Digital Social Connections

Chapter 1: Understanding Digital Social Connections

The digital age has fundamentally reshaped how we connect, communicate, and build relationships. The rise of social media platforms has created a virtual landscape where individuals can interact with others across geographical boundaries, fostering communities and sharing experiences in unprecedented ways. This chapter delves into the evolution of digital social connections, exploring the impact of social media, the concept of digital identity, the dynamics of online relationships, the importance of authenticity, and the potential future of digital socializing.

The Rise of Social Media:

The advent of social media marked a paradigm shift in human interaction. Platforms like Facebook, Twitter, Instagram, and TikTok have become integral parts of our daily lives, offering avenues for self-expression, information sharing, and social networking. These platforms have democratized communication, enabling individuals to share their thoughts, experiences, and perspectives with a global audience. The rise of social media has also facilitated the formation of online communities centered around shared interests, hobbies, or causes, connecting individuals who might not have otherwise crossed paths.

The proliferation of social media has not been without its drawbacks. Concerns have been raised regarding data privacy, the spread of misinformation, and the potential for online harassment. The addictive nature of these platforms and their impact on mental health are also subjects of ongoing discussion. Despite these challenges, social media continues to evolve, shaping the way we interact and consume information.

The Role of Digital Identity:

In the digital realm, individuals cultivate a digital identity, a representation of themselves constructed through online profiles, posts, and interactions. This digital identity can be a curated version of one's offline persona, highlighting certain aspects while downplaying others. The concept of digital identity raises questions about authenticity and the potential for individuals to misrepresent themselves online.

The distinction between one's digital and physical identities is often blurred. While some individuals strive to maintain consistency between their online and offline personas, others adopt different identities in virtual spaces. This can be a form of self-expression or a way to explore different facets of one's personality. However, it also raises ethical considerations about the potential for deception and the impact on online trust.

Digital vs. Physical Social Networks:

While digital social networks offer convenience and accessibility, they differ from physical social networks in several key aspects. Physical interactions involve nonverbal cues, such as body language and facial expressions, which contribute to a richer understanding of communication. Digital interactions, on the other hand, rely primarily on text, images, and videos, which can lead to misinterpretations and misunderstandings.

The level of intimacy and depth in relationships also differs between digital and physical social networks. While online platforms can facilitate the formation of new connections, building deep, meaningful relationships often requires face-to-face interaction and shared experiences. The ephemeral nature of some online interactions can also hinder the development of lasting bonds.

Psychological Impact of Online Relationships:

The pervasive use of social media has had a profound impact on our psychological well-being. While online platforms can provide a sense of connection and belonging, they can also contribute to feelings of isolation, anxiety, and depression. The constant exposure to curated online personas can lead to social comparison and feelings of inadequacy.

The validation-seeking nature of social media can also impact self-esteem. The number of likes, comments, and followers can become a metric for self-worth, leading to a preoccupation with online approval. The fear of missing out (FOMO) can also contribute to anxiety and a sense of pressure to constantly be connected.

Authenticity in Online Interactions:

In a digital landscape where curated personas are commonplace, authenticity is becoming increasingly valued. Being genuine and transparent in online interactions fosters trust and builds stronger connections. Authenticity involves expressing one's true self, sharing personal experiences, and engaging in honest conversations.

The pressure to conform to online norms and present a perfect image can hinder authenticity. However, embracing vulnerability and imperfections can foster deeper connections and create a sense of shared humanity. Authenticity also involves being mindful of the information shared online and ensuring that it aligns with one's values and beliefs.

The Future of Digital Socializing:

The landscape of digital socializing is constantly evolving. Emerging technologies, such as virtual reality and augmented reality, are blurring the lines between the physical and digital worlds, creating new possibilities for social interaction. The metaverse, a persistent virtual world, holds the potential to transform how we connect, communicate, and build communities.

The future of digital socializing will likely involve a greater emphasis on personalized experiences and immersive technologies. Artificial intelligence will play an increasingly important role in shaping online interactions, offering personalized recommendations and facilitating communication. As digital socializing continues to evolve, it will be crucial to address ethical considerations and ensure that these technologies are used responsibly to foster positive and meaningful connections.

Chapter 2: Setting Up for Success in the Digital World

Navigating the digital world requires a strategic approach to building a strong and positive online presence. This chapter outlines essential steps for establishing a successful online presence, covering topics such as choosing the right platforms, creating a consistent online identity, defining your digital voice, optimizing privacy settings, navigating digital etiquette, and establishing boundaries in online spaces.

Choosing the Right Platforms:

The first step in establishing a digital presence is selecting the platforms that align with your goals and target audience. Each platform has its own unique features, demographics, and cultural norms. For example, LinkedIn is geared towards professional networking, while Instagram focuses on visual content and community building. Choosing the right platforms allows you to connect with the right people and maximize your impact.

Consider your target audience and the type of content you plan to share when selecting platforms. Research the demographics of each platform and analyze the engagement levels of similar accounts. Focus your efforts on a few key platforms rather than spreading yourself too thin across multiple channels.

Creating a Consistent Online Identity:

Consistency is crucial for building a recognizable and trustworthy online presence. Maintain a consistent profile picture, username, and bio across different platforms. This creates a cohesive brand identity and makes it easier for people to recognize and connect with you.

Consistency also extends to the type of content you share. Establish a clear theme or focus for your online presence and create content that aligns with your brand identity. Consistency in your messaging and visual style builds trust and reinforces your expertise.

Defining Your Digital Voice:

Your digital voice is the unique way you communicate and express yourself online. It reflects your personality, values, and expertise. Defining your digital voice helps you connect with your audience on a deeper level and establish a distinct online presence.

Consider your target audience and the message you want to convey when crafting your digital voice. Use language that resonates with your audience and reflects your brand identity. Be authentic and genuine in your communication, and avoid trying to imitate others.

Optimizing Privacy Settings:

Protecting your privacy online is essential for safeguarding your personal information and maintaining a positive online presence. Familiarize yourself with the privacy settings on each platform and adjust them to control who can see your content and interact with you.

Limit the visibility of sensitive information, such as your phone number, email address, and home address. Be mindful of the information you share publicly and avoid posting anything that could compromise your safety or reputation. Regularly review and update your privacy settings as platforms evolve.

Navigating Digital Etiquette:

Digital etiquette encompasses the norms and behaviors that govern online interaction. Being respectful, considerate, and mindful of others is crucial for building positive online relationships. Avoid engaging in online harassment, cyberbullying, or spreading misinformation.

Be mindful of the language you use and avoid using offensive or inflammatory language. Respect others' opinions and engage in constructive dialogue. Be aware of cultural differences and avoid making assumptions about others' backgrounds or beliefs.

Establishing Boundaries in Online Spaces:

Setting boundaries in online spaces is essential for maintaining a healthy relationship with technology and protecting your mental well-being. Establish clear guidelines for how much time you spend online and what type of content you consume.

Limit your exposure to negative or triggering content. Take breaks from social media regularly to recharge and reconnect with the offline world. Be selective about who you interact with online and avoid engaging with individuals who exhibit toxic behavior. Establish clear communication boundaries with online connections and be assertive about your needs and expectations.

By following these guidelines, individuals can cultivate a positive and impactful online presence, leveraging the power of digital platforms to connect, communicate, and build meaningful relationships. A well-defined online presence can open doors to new opportunities, foster professional growth, and enhance personal connections in the digital age.

Chapter 3: Building an Online Presence from Scratch

Creating a compelling online presence involves more than simply signing up for social media accounts. It requires a strategic approach to crafting a personal brand, developing engaging content, and leveraging the power of visual storytelling. This chapter provides a comprehensive guide to building an online presence from the ground up, covering essential elements such as developing a personal brand, crafting engaging content, and harnessing the power of visual storytelling.

Developing a Personal Brand:

Your personal brand is the unique combination of skills, experiences, and values that define you online. It's how you present yourself to the digital world and what sets you apart from others. A strong personal brand can enhance your professional prospects, attract new opportunities, and build credibility in your field.

Start by identifying your strengths, passions, and areas of expertise. What unique value do you offer? What message do you want to convey to your audience? Develop a clear brand statement that encapsulates your essence and communicates your value proposition. Consistency is key to building a strong personal brand. Maintain a cohesive message and visual style across all your online platforms.

Crafting Engaging Content:

Content is the lifeblood of any online presence. Creating high-quality, engaging content that resonates with your target audience is essential for building a loyal following and establishing yourself as a thought leader. Content can take many forms, including blog posts, articles, videos, infographics, and social media updates.

Focus on creating content that provides value to your audience. Educate, entertain, or inspire them. Share your expertise, insights, and experiences. Ask questions, encourage interaction, and build a sense of community. Experiment with different content formats to see what resonates best with your audience.

The Power of Visual Storytelling:

Visuals are a powerful tool for capturing attention and conveying complex information in a concise and engaging manner. Images, videos, and graphics can enhance your storytelling, evoke emotions, and create a lasting impression. Incorporate visuals into your content strategy to elevate your online presence and connect with your audience on a deeper level.

Use high-quality images and videos that are relevant to your message. Optimize visuals for different platforms and devices. Experiment with different visual styles to find what best represents your brand. Use captions and descriptions to provide context and enhance the storytelling experience.

Building a Content Strategy:

Creating a content strategy provides a roadmap for your online presence. A well-defined strategy helps you stay organized, maintain consistency, and achieve your goals. Start by defining your target audience and understanding their needs and interests. What type of content will resonate with them? What platforms do they use?

Develop a content calendar to schedule and organize your content creation efforts. This helps you maintain a consistent posting schedule and ensures that you have a variety of content to share. Track your content performance and analyze the data to see what's working and what's not. Adjust your strategy based on the insights you gather.

Building a Website or Portfolio:

A website or online portfolio provides a central hub for your online presence. It's a place where you can showcase your work, share your story, and connect with your audience. A well-designed website can enhance your credibility, attract new opportunities, and serve as a valuable resource for your followers.

Choose a domain name that reflects your brand and is easy to remember. Create a user-friendly website that is easy to navigate and visually appealing. Showcase your best work and highlight your accomplishments. Include a blog or news section to share updates and engage with your audience. Optimize your website for search engines to improve its visibility.

Building an online presence takes time, effort, and consistency. By focusing on crafting a compelling personal brand, creating engaging content, and leveraging the power of visual storytelling, individuals can establish a strong and impactful online presence that enhances their personal and professional lives.

Chapter 4: Engaging with Digital Communities

Building a robust online presence extends beyond simply broadcasting your message; it thrives on active participation and engagement within digital communities. This chapter delves into the strategies and nuances of effectively engaging with online communities, covering topics such as finding and joining relevant groups, participating in discussions, building relationships with influencers, supporting others in online spaces, the importance of giving back, and managing online conflict.

Finding and Joining Relevant Groups:

The digital landscape is teeming with communities centered around shared interests, professions, hobbies, and causes. Identifying and joining relevant groups allows you to connect with like-minded individuals, expand your network, and participate in meaningful conversations.

Utilize platform-specific search features to discover groups related to your interests. Explore hashtags and keywords related to your niche. Research online directories and forums. Consider your goals for joining a group. Are you seeking professional connections, support, or simply a sense of community? Choose groups that align with your objectives.

Participating in Discussions:

Active participation in discussions is essential for establishing your presence within a digital community. Contribute thoughtful comments, share insightful perspectives, and engage in respectful dialogue with other members. Avoid self-promotion or spamming the group with irrelevant content.

Listen actively to what others are saying and respond thoughtfully. Ask questions to encourage further discussion. Offer support and encouragement to other members. Share relevant resources and information. Be respectful of differing opinions and avoid engaging in personal attacks.

Building Relationships with Influencers:

Influencers are individuals who have established a significant following and credibility within a specific niche. Building relationships with influencers can expand your reach, introduce you to new audiences, and enhance your credibility.

Engage with influencers' content by liking, commenting, and sharing their posts. Participate in discussions they initiate. Offer genuine compliments and acknowledge their expertise. Avoid bombarding them with requests or self-promotional messages. Focus on building a genuine connection based on mutual respect and shared interests.

Supporting Others in Online Spaces:

Supporting others in online communities fosters a sense of camaraderie and strengthens relationships. Offer encouragement, celebrate successes, and provide assistance when needed. Building a supportive online presence strengthens your reputation and creates a positive environment for everyone.

Share others' content and promote their work. Offer constructive feedback and provide helpful suggestions. Celebrate milestones and achievements. Offer support during challenging times. Be a positive and encouraging presence in the community.

The Importance of Giving Back:

Contributing to the community through acts of service or sharing valuable resources enhances your online presence and builds goodwill. Giving back can take many forms, such as offering free advice, creating helpful tutorials, or volunteering your time.

Identify areas where you can contribute your expertise and skills. Offer free webinars or online workshops. Create and share valuable resources, such as checklists, templates, or ebooks. Support charitable causes and organizations. Participate in community events and initiatives.

Managing Online Conflict:

Disagreements and conflicts are inevitable in online communities. Managing conflict effectively requires diplomacy, empathy, and a commitment to respectful communication. Avoid engaging in personal attacks or inflammatory language.

Listen actively to understand the other person's perspective. Acknowledge their feelings and validate their concerns. Focus on finding common ground and seeking mutually acceptable solutions. If the conflict escalates, disengage from the conversation and report the behavior to the community moderators.

By actively engaging with digital communities, individuals can build valuable relationships, expand their networks, and establish a strong online presence. Participating in discussions, supporting others, and giving back fosters a sense of belonging and strengthens the overall community. Managing online conflict effectively ensures a positive and productive online experience for everyone.

Chapter 5: Strengthening Digital Relationships

While initiating connections in the digital realm is relatively easy, nurturing and strengthening those relationships requires dedicated effort and a nuanced understanding of online dynamics. This chapter explores key strategies for fostering deeper and more meaningful digital relationships, focusing on building trust, active listening, constructive feedback, personalized communication, celebrating milestones, and overcoming communication barriers.

Fostering Trust in Digital Spaces:

Trust is the bedrock of any strong relationship, and digital spaces are no exception. Building trust online requires transparency, authenticity, and consistent positive engagement. Be truthful in your interactions, share your experiences genuinely, and demonstrate respect for others' perspectives.

Follow through on your commitments and be reliable. Maintain confidentiality and respect others' privacy. Be open to feedback and willing to acknowledge mistakes. Demonstrate empathy and understanding in your interactions. Consistency in your online behavior builds trust over time.

The Importance of Active Listening:

Active listening is crucial for fostering understanding and building rapport in digital communication. It involves paying close attention to what others are saying, both verbally and nonverbally (through written cues), and responding thoughtfully. Avoid interrupting or dominating the conversation.

Ask clarifying questions to ensure understanding. Summarize key points to demonstrate that you are actively engaged.

Acknowledge others' feelings and validate their experiences. Avoid distractions and focus on the conversation at hand. Active listening demonstrates respect and fosters deeper connection.

Giving Constructive Feedback:

Providing constructive feedback is essential for growth and development in digital relationships, whether personal or professional. Focus on specific behaviors and their impact, rather than making generalizations or personal attacks. Frame feedback positively and offer suggestions for improvement.

Begin by acknowledging the positive aspects of the situation. Be specific in your feedback and provide concrete examples. Focus on the behavior, not the person. Offer actionable suggestions for improvement. Frame feedback as an opportunity for growth and development.

Personalizing Communication:

In a world increasingly dominated by automated messages and generic interactions, personalized communication stands out. Tailoring your messages to the individual demonstrates genuine interest and strengthens the connection. Take the time to learn about the other person's interests and preferences.

Use their name in your communication. Reference previous conversations or shared experiences. Tailor your message to their specific needs and interests. Offer personalized recommendations or resources. Small gestures of personalization can make a big difference in building rapport.

Celebrating Milestones Together:

Celebrating milestones and achievements, both big and small, strengthens bonds and fosters a sense of shared joy in digital relationships. Acknowledge birthdays, anniversaries, professional accomplishments, and personal victories. Show your support and celebrate their success.

Send congratulatory messages or virtual gifts. Share their accomplishments on social media. Offer words of encouragement and support. Celebrating milestones together strengthens the sense of community and reinforces positive relationships.

Overcoming Digital Communication Barriers:

Digital communication can present unique challenges, such as misinterpretations, language barriers, and technical difficulties. Overcoming these barriers requires patience, understanding, and a willingness to adapt.

Be clear and concise in your communication. Avoid using jargon or technical terms that may not be understood by everyone. Use emojis and emoticons judiciously to convey tone and emotion. Be mindful of cultural differences in communication styles. If miscommunication occurs, clarify your message and seek to understand the other person's perspective.

Strengthening digital relationships requires conscious effort and a commitment to fostering trust, active listening, and personalized communication. By embracing these strategies, individuals can build deeper connections, foster meaningful interactions, and cultivate a supportive and enriching online experience. Celebrating milestones together and overcoming communication barriers further strengthens these bonds and fosters a sense of belonging in the digital world.

Chapter 6: Measuring the Impact of Your Digital Presence

Establishing a digital presence is not merely about existing online; it's about making a meaningful impact. This chapter delves into the crucial aspect of measuring the effectiveness of your digital endeavors, encompassing key metrics, analytical tools, and strategic adjustments based on data insights. It also covers the importance of monitoring brand sentiment and adapting strategies for long-term growth.

Key Metrics to Track Success:

Measuring the success of your digital presence requires identifying and tracking key performance indicators (KPIs) that align with your goals. These metrics provide quantifiable data that reflects the effectiveness of your strategies. Different platforms offer various analytics dashboards, providing valuable insights into audience engagement, content performance, and overall reach.

- **Reach:** Measures the number of unique individuals exposed to your content. A broader reach indicates greater visibility and potential for engagement.
- **Engagement:** Encompasses various interactions with your content, such as likes, comments, shares, and clicks. High engagement signifies audience interest and resonance.
- **Website Traffic:** Tracks the number of visitors to your website, providing insights into the effectiveness of your content marketing and SEO strategies.
- **Conversion Rate:** Measures the percentage of visitors who complete a desired action, such as making a purchase, signing up for a newsletter, or filling out a

form. A high conversion rate indicates effective targeting and compelling content.

- **Follower Growth:** Monitors the growth of your audience across various platforms, reflecting the effectiveness of your community-building efforts.

Understanding Engagement Rates:

Engagement rates represent the level of interaction your content receives relative to your audience size. High engagement rates suggest that your content resonates with your audience, while low engagement may indicate a need for strategic adjustments.

Calculate engagement rates by dividing the total number of engagements (likes, comments, shares) by your reach or follower count. Compare your engagement rates to industry benchmarks and analyze trends over time. Identify content formats and topics that generate higher engagement and adjust your strategy accordingly.

The Role of Analytics Tools:

Various analytics tools provide in-depth data and insights to help you understand your audience, track performance, and optimize your strategies. Platform-specific analytics dashboards offer valuable information about audience demographics, engagement patterns, and content performance.

- **Google Analytics:** Provides comprehensive data on website traffic, user behavior, and conversion rates.
- **Social Media Analytics Dashboards:** Offer platform-specific insights into audience demographics, engagement metrics, and content performance.
- **Third-Party Analytics Tools:** Offer advanced features such as competitive analysis, keyword research, and social listening.

Adjusting Strategies Based on Data:

Data-driven decision-making is essential for optimizing your digital presence. Analyze the data gathered from various analytics tools to identify trends, patterns, and areas for improvement. Adjust your content strategy, platform focus, and engagement tactics based on these insights.

If certain content formats or topics are performing poorly, consider revising your approach or exploring alternative strategies. If engagement rates are declining, experiment with different engagement tactics or explore new platforms. Continuously analyze data and adapt your strategies to stay ahead of the curve.

Monitoring Brand Sentiment:

Monitoring brand sentiment involves tracking public opinion and perception of your brand online. This includes analyzing social media conversations, reviews, and mentions to understand how your audience feels about your brand, products, or services.

Use social listening tools to track brand mentions and analyze the sentiment expressed in online conversations. Address negative feedback promptly and professionally. Engage in positive interactions with your audience to build trust and strengthen relationships. Monitoring brand sentiment provides valuable insights for reputation management and brand building.

Long-Term Growth Strategies:

Building a sustainable digital presence requires a long-term perspective and a commitment to continuous improvement. Develop a long-term growth strategy that aligns with your overall goals and incorporates data-driven insights.

- **Diversify your content:** Explore different content formats and topics to keep your audience engaged and attract new followers.
- **Expand your reach:** Explore new platforms and communities to reach a wider audience.
- **Build relationships:** Foster meaningful connections with influencers and other key players in your industry.
- **Stay updated:** Keep abreast of the latest trends and technologies in the digital landscape.
- **Adapt and evolve:** Continuously analyze data and adjust your strategies to stay ahead of the curve.

By diligently tracking key metrics, leveraging analytics tools, and adapting strategies based on data insights, individuals and businesses can maximize the impact of their digital presence. Monitoring brand sentiment and implementing long-term growth strategies ensures sustained success in the ever-evolving digital landscape.

Part 2:

Content Creation and Strategy

Chapter 1: Developing a Content Strategy

In the bustling digital landscape, a well-defined content strategy serves as a compass, guiding your efforts and ensuring your message resonates with the right audience. This chapter delves into the crucial elements of developing a robust content strategy, covering topics such as defining your goals and audience, establishing content pillars and themes, mapping your content calendar, balancing promotional and valuable content, experimenting with formats, and tracking content performance.

Defining Your Goals and Audience:

Before embarking on content creation, it's essential to establish clear goals. What do you hope to achieve with your content? Are you aiming to increase brand awareness, drive website traffic, generate leads, or build a community? Clearly defined goals provide direction and purpose.

Equally important is understanding your target audience. Who are you trying to reach? What are their interests, needs, and pain points? Conduct thorough audience research to gain insights into their demographics, online behavior, and preferred content formats. Creating audience personas can be helpful in visualizing and understanding your target audience.

Content Pillars and Themes:

Content pillars are the core topics or themes that form the foundation of your content strategy. These pillars should align with your brand identity, target audience interests, and overall goals. Establishing content pillars provides structure and consistency to your content creation efforts.

Choose three to five core pillars that represent your area of expertise or the key themes you want to address. These pillars should be broad enough to encompass a variety of content ideas, yet specific enough to maintain focus and avoid diluting your message. For example, a fitness brand might choose pillars such as nutrition, workout routines, and mindset.

Mapping Your Content Calendar:

A content calendar is a valuable tool for organizing and scheduling your content creation and distribution efforts. It provides a visual overview of your planned content, ensuring a consistent posting schedule and a diverse mix of topics. A content calendar can be a simple spreadsheet or a more sophisticated software solution.

Plan your content in advance, taking into account key dates, events, and seasonal trends. Map out your content pillars and themes across different platforms and formats. Schedule specific publishing dates and times to maintain consistency. A content calendar helps you stay organized and ensures a steady flow of engaging content.

Balancing Promotional and Value Content:

While promoting your products or services is important, providing valuable content that educates, entertains, or informs your audience is crucial for building trust and establishing long-term relationships. Strive for a balance between promotional and value-driven content.

The 80/20 rule is a good guideline: 80% of your content should provide value to your audience, while 20% can be promotional. Focus on creating content that addresses your audience's needs and interests. Provide helpful tips, insightful advice, and entertaining stories. Promotional content should be integrated seamlessly and provide genuine value.

Experimenting with Formats:

Different content formats cater to different audience preferences and consumption habits. Experimenting with various formats, such as blog posts, videos, infographics, podcasts, and social media updates, allows you to reach a wider audience and keep your content fresh and engaging.

Consider your target audience's preferred content formats. Analyze the performance of different formats to see what resonates best with your audience. Repurpose existing content into different formats to maximize its reach and impact. For example, a blog post can be transformed into a video, infographic, or series of social media updates.

Tracking Content Performance:

Tracking content performance is crucial for understanding what resonates with your audience and optimizing your strategy. Utilize analytics tools to monitor key metrics such as reach, engagement, website traffic, and conversion rates.

Analyze the data to identify trends, patterns, and areas for improvement. Which content formats are performing best? Which topics are generating the most engagement? Use these insights to refine your content strategy and create more effective content. Regularly review and adjust your strategy based on data analysis.

Developing a robust content strategy is the cornerstone of a successful digital presence. By defining clear goals, understanding your audience, establishing content pillars, utilizing a content calendar, balancing promotional and valuable content, experimenting with formats, and tracking performance, you can create a compelling online presence that engages your target audience and achieves your desired outcomes. Remember that content strategy is an iterative process; continuous monitoring, analysis, and adaptation are key to long-term success.

Chapter 2: Creating Value-Driven Content

In the crowded digital arena, capturing and retaining audience attention requires more than just posting content; it demands offering genuine value. This chapter explores the art of crafting value-driven content that resonates with your target audience, fostering engagement, and building lasting relationships. We'll delve into various content formats and strategies, including crafting informative blog posts, harnessing the power of tutorials and how-to guides, utilizing interactive content like polls and surveys, incorporating storytelling techniques, curating and sharing relevant content, and leveraging user-generated content.

Crafting Informative Blog Posts:

Blog posts provide a versatile platform for sharing in-depth knowledge, insights, and perspectives on topics relevant to your audience. Well-researched and engaging blog posts can establish you as a thought leader, drive website traffic, and nurture leads.

- **Focus on a specific topic:** Each blog post should address a particular subject thoroughly, providing valuable information and insights.
- **Conduct thorough research:** Back up your claims with credible sources and data to enhance your credibility.
- **Use clear and concise language:** Write in a style that is easy to understand and engaging for your target audience.
- **Optimize for search engines (SEO):** Incorporate relevant keywords and phrases to improve your search engine ranking and visibility.
- **Include visuals:** Break up large blocks of text with images, videos, and infographics to enhance readability and engagement.

The Power of Tutorials and How-To Guides:

Tutorials and how-to guides provide practical, step-by-step instructions that empower your audience to learn new skills or solve specific problems. These content formats are highly valuable and can generate significant engagement.

- **Identify a common problem:** Focus on addressing a challenge that your target audience frequently faces.
- **Break down the solution into steps:** Provide clear and concise instructions, using visuals and examples to illustrate each step.
- **Use a variety of formats:** Create video tutorials, written guides, or interactive walkthroughs to cater to different learning styles.
- **Encourage interaction:** Invite users to ask questions, share their experiences, and provide feedback.

Interactive Content: Polls and Surveys:

Interactive content, such as polls and surveys, encourages active participation from your audience, providing valuable insights into their preferences and opinions while boosting engagement.

- **Ask engaging questions:** Pose questions that arc relevant to your audience and encourage thoughtful responses.
- **Use a variety of formats:** Create multiple-choice polls, open-ended surveys, quizzes, and interactive games.
- **Share the results:** Share the aggregated results with your audience to foster transparency and encourage further discussion.
- **Use data to inform future content:** Analyze the data gathered from polls and surveys to understand your audience better and tailor your content accordingly.

Using Storytelling to Engage:

Storytelling is a powerful tool for connecting with your audience on an emotional level. Weaving narratives into your content can make it more memorable, relatable, and impactful.

- **Craft compelling narratives:** Develop stories that resonate with your audience's values, aspirations, and experiences.
- **Use relatable characters:** Create characters that your audience can identify with and root for.
- **Highlight emotions:** Evoke emotions such as joy, sadness, or inspiration to create a deeper connection with your audience.
- **Incorporate visuals:** Use images and videos to enhance the storytelling experience and bring your narratives to life.

Content Curation and Sharing:

Sharing relevant and valuable content from other sources complements your original content and positions you as a knowledgeable resource within your niche.

- **Curate high-quality content:** Share articles, videos, and other resources that are relevant to your audience and align with your brand values.
- **Provide context:** Add your own insights and commentary when sharing curated content to add value and personalize the experience.
- **Credit the original source:** Always attribute the content to the original creator to maintain ethical practices and build relationships.

Leveraging User-Generated Content:

User-generated content (UGC) is content created by your audience, such as reviews, testimonials, photos, and videos. Leveraging UGC can enhance your brand credibility, build community, and provide valuable social proof.

- **Encourage UGC creation:** Run contests, challenges, or campaigns that encourage your audience to create and share content related to your brand.
- **Showcase UGC:** Feature user-generated content on your website, social media channels, and other marketing materials.
- **Give credit and recognition:** Always acknowledge and thank users for their contributions.

By focusing on creating valuable, engaging, and diverse content, you can establish a strong online presence that resonates with your target audience, fosters meaningful connections, and achieves your desired outcomes. Remember that content creation is an ongoing process; continuous experimentation, analysis, and adaptation are essential for staying relevant and impactful in the dynamic digital landscape.

Chapter 3: Visual Content Mastery

In the visually-driven digital landscape, mastering the art of visual content is no longer optional; it's a necessity. This chapter delves into the essential elements of creating compelling visuals that capture attention, communicate effectively, and enhance your online presence. We'll explore various aspects of visual content creation, including designing compelling graphics, mastering photography for social media, engaging audiences with video content, leveraging the power of live streaming, incorporating infographics effectively, and maintaining visual consistency across platforms.

Designing Compelling Graphics:

Graphics encompass a wide range of visual elements, including images, illustrations, icons, and typography. Well-designed graphics can enhance your brand identity, communicate complex information concisely, and elevate the overall aesthetic of your online presence.

- **Utilize design principles:** Employ principles of design, such as color theory, typography, and composition, to create visually appealing and balanced graphics.
- **Maintain brand consistency:** Use consistent colors, fonts, and imagery that align with your brand guidelines to reinforce your brand identity.
- **Choose appropriate file formats:** Select file formats optimized for different platforms and purposes. For example, use PNG for graphics with transparent backgrounds and JPEG for photographs.
- **Optimize for different devices:** Ensure your graphics display correctly on various screen sizes and resolutions.

The Art of Photography for Social Media:

High-quality photography can significantly enhance your social media presence, capturing attention and conveying emotions effectively.

- **Invest in good equipment:** While smartphone cameras are increasingly capable, consider investing in a dedicated camera for professional-quality images.
- **Master composition techniques:** Learn basic photography principles, such as the rule of thirds and leading lines, to create visually appealing compositions.
- **Use natural lighting:** Natural light is generally more flattering than artificial light. Shoot outdoors or near a window whenever possible.
- **Edit your photos:** Use editing software to enhance your photos, adjust lighting, and correct imperfections.

Video Content: Engaging Audiences:

Video has become a dominant force in online content consumption. Creating engaging video content can significantly boost your reach, engagement, and brand awareness.

- **Plan your videos:** Develop a clear concept and script before filming to ensure a cohesive and impactful message.
- **Invest in quality audio and video:** Poor audio quality can detract from even the most visually appealing videos. Invest in a good microphone and ensure adequate lighting.
- **Keep it concise:** Attention spans are short online. Keep your videos concise and to the point.
- **Add captions and subtitles:** Many users watch videos without sound. Adding captions and subtitles makes your content accessible to a wider audience.

Live Streaming and Real-Time Engagement:

Live streaming offers a unique opportunity to connect with your audience in real-time, fostering a sense of community and immediacy.

- **Choose the right platform:** Different platforms cater to different audiences and purposes. Select a platform that aligns with your goals and target audience.
- **Promote your live streams in advance:** Announce your live streams ahead of time to generate anticipation and maximize viewership.
- **Interact with your audience:** Respond to comments and questions in real-time to foster engagement and build relationships.
- **Repurpose your live streams:** After the live stream ends, repurpose the recording into shorter clips or other content formats.

Incorporating Infographics:

Infographics are a powerful tool for presenting complex information in a visually appealing and easily digestible format.

- **Focus on a specific topic:** Each infographic should address a particular subject thoroughly, providing valuable data and insights.
- **Use clear and concise language:** Present information in a way that is easy to understand and avoids jargon.
- **Use visuals effectively:** Combine charts, graphs, icons, and illustrations to enhance understanding and engagement.
- **Cite your sources:** Provide attribution for any data or statistics used in your infographic.

Visual Consistency Across Platforms:

Maintaining visual consistency across different platforms reinforces your brand identity and creates a cohesive online presence.

- **Develop brand guidelines:** Establish clear guidelines for your visual identity, including colors, fonts, logo usage, and imagery.
- **Use consistent profile pictures and cover photos:** Ensure your profile visuals are consistent across all platforms.
- **Apply consistent filters and editing styles:** Maintain a consistent aesthetic in your photos and videos.

By mastering the art of visual content creation, you can elevate your online presence, capture attention, communicate effectively, and build stronger connections with your audience. Remember that visual content trends evolve constantly; staying updated on the latest techniques and technologies is essential for remaining competitive in the digital landscape.

Chapter 4: Content Marketing and Promotion

Creating compelling content is only half the battle; effectively promoting it to reach your target audience is equally crucial. This chapter explores the strategies and tactics of content marketing and promotion, encompassing organic reach, paid advertising, email marketing, influencer collaborations, cross-platform promotion, contests and giveaways, and leveraging SEO for social media. We'll delve into each of these areas, providing insights and best practices for maximizing your content's impact.

Organic vs. Paid Promotion:

Organic promotion relies on building a loyal following and engaging with your audience through valuable content and authentic interactions. Paid promotion involves investing in advertising to reach a wider audience and amplify your message. Both approaches have their merits and can be used effectively in conjunction.

- **Organic Promotion:** Focus on creating high-quality content that resonates with your target audience. Engage in conversations, respond to comments, and build relationships. Participate in relevant online communities.
- **Paid Promotion:** Utilize social media advertising platforms and search engine marketing to target specific demographics and interests. Experiment with different ad formats and targeting options to optimize your campaigns.

Building an Email Marketing Strategy:

Email marketing remains a powerful tool for nurturing leads, building relationships, and promoting your content directly to your subscribers' inboxes.

- **Build an email list:** Offer valuable incentives, such as free ebooks, checklists, or exclusive content, in exchange for email sign-ups.
- **Segment your audience:** Divide your email list into segments based on demographics, interests, or purchase history to personalize your messaging.
- **Create engaging email content:** Craft compelling subject lines, personalize your emails, and provide valuable information that resonates with your subscribers.
- **Track your results:** Monitor key metrics such as open rates, click-through rates, and conversion rates to optimize your email campaigns.

Collaborating with Influencers:

Influencer marketing involves partnering with individuals who have a significant following and influence within your target audience. Collaborations can expand your reach, introduce you to new audiences, and enhance your credibility.

- **Identify relevant influencers:** Research influencers whose audience aligns with your target market and whose values align with your brand.
- **Develop mutually beneficial partnerships:** Create campaigns that benefit both you and the influencer. Offer fair compensation and creative freedom.
- **Track the results of your collaborations:** Monitor key metrics such as reach, engagement, and website traffic

to measure the effectiveness of your influencer marketing campaigns.

Cross-Promoting on Multiple Platforms:

Leveraging multiple platforms expands your reach and reinforces your message. Cross-promote your content across different social media channels, your website, and email marketing to maximize visibility.

- **Tailor your message for each platform:** Adapt your content to suit the specific format and culture of each platform.
- **Use platform-specific features:** Utilize hashtags, stories, and live streams to engage your audience on different platforms.
- **Track the performance of each platform:** Analyze data to understand which platforms are most effective for reaching your target audience.

Running Contests and Giveaways:

Contests and giveaways can generate excitement, boost engagement, and attract new followers.

- **Set clear goals:** Determine what you want to achieve with your contest or giveaway, such as increasing brand awareness, generating leads, or driving sales.
- **Choose relevant prizes:** Offer prizes that appeal to your target audience and align with your brand.
- **Promote your contest or giveaway widely:** Use social media, email marketing, and other channels to spread the word.
- **Follow up with participants:** Engage with participants after the contest or giveaway ends to nurture relationships.

Leveraging SEO for Social Media:

Optimizing your social media profiles and content for search engines can improve your visibility and attract new followers.

- **Use relevant keywords:** Incorporate keywords and phrases that are relevant to your industry and target audience.
- **Optimize your profile descriptions:** Craft compelling profile descriptions that accurately reflect your brand and include relevant keywords.
- **Use hashtags strategically:** Research relevant hashtags and use them sparingly to improve discoverability.

By implementing a comprehensive content marketing and promotion strategy, encompassing both organic and paid methods, email marketing, influencer collaborations, cross-platform promotion, contests and giveaways, and SEO optimization, you can effectively amplify your message, reach a wider audience, and achieve your marketing objectives. Remember to continuously analyze your results and adapt your strategies to stay ahead of the curve in the ever-evolving digital landscape.

Chapter 5: Storytelling for Connection

In the digital age, where attention spans are fleeting and content overload is rampant, the ability to connect with your audience on an emotional level is paramount. This chapter explores the power of storytelling as a tool for building authentic connections, fostering engagement, and driving meaningful impact. We'll delve into the core principles of narrative structure, emotional storytelling techniques, crafting personal stories, adapting storytelling for brands and businesses, creating episodic content, and inspiring action through compelling narratives.

Understanding the Power of Narrative:

Stories are fundamental to human communication. They provide a framework for understanding the world, connecting with others, and transmitting values and beliefs. Harnessing the power of narrative in your content allows you to engage your audience on a deeper level, making your message more memorable and impactful.

- **Structure:** Effective stories follow a narrative arc, with a beginning, rising action, climax, falling action, and resolution. This structure creates anticipation and provides a satisfying conclusion.
- **Character:** Compelling characters, whether real or fictional, draw the audience into the story and allow them to connect with the narrative on a personal level.
- **Conflict:** Conflict drives the narrative forward, creating tension and keeping the audience engaged. Conflict can be internal or external, and its resolution provides a sense of closure.
- **Theme:** The underlying message or theme of the story provides meaning and resonance. Themes can explore

universal human experiences, such as love, loss, or overcoming adversity.

Sharing Personal Stories:

Sharing personal anecdotes and experiences can create a sense of authenticity and vulnerability, allowing your audience to connect with you on a human level.

- **Be authentic:** Share genuine experiences and emotions. Avoid embellishing or fabricating stories.
- **Focus on the takeaway:** What lesson or insight did you gain from the experience? What message do you want to convey to your audience?
- **Be mindful of your audience:** Consider the appropriateness of your story for your target audience and the platform you are using.

Storytelling for Brands and Businesses:

Storytelling can be a powerful tool for brands and businesses to connect with their customers, build brand loyalty, and drive sales.

- **Develop a brand narrative:** Craft a compelling story that encapsulates your brand's values, mission, and history.
- **Connect with your audience's values:** Tell stories that resonate with your target audience's aspirations, beliefs, and experiences.
- **Showcase customer stories:** Share testimonials, case studies, and user-generated content to build trust and social proof.
- **Use storytelling in marketing campaigns:** Integrate storytelling into your advertising, social media content,

and email marketing to engage your audience and drive conversions.

Emotional Storytelling Techniques:

Evoking emotions through your storytelling can create a deeper connection with your audience and make your message more memorable.

- **Use vivid language:** Employ descriptive language and sensory details to paint a picture in the reader's mind.
- **Show, don't tell:** Use actions, dialogue, and imagery to convey emotions rather than simply stating them.
- **Focus on the human element:** Highlight the human impact of your story to create empathy and connection.

Creating Episodic Content:

Episodic content, such as a series of blog posts, videos, or podcasts, allows you to develop a narrative over time, building anticipation and keeping your audience engaged.

- **Develop a overarching narrative:** Create a central storyline that connects each episode.
- **Introduce cliffhangers:** End each episode with a cliffhanger to encourage viewers to tune in for the next installment.
- **Create recurring characters:** Develop relatable characters that your audience can connect with over time.

Inspiring Action through Stories:

Stories can be a powerful call to action, inspiring your audience to take specific steps, such as making a purchase, signing up for a newsletter, or supporting a cause.

- **Clearly define your call to action:** What do you want your audience to do after reading or watching your story?
- **Connect the call to action to the narrative:** Make sure the call to action flows naturally from the story and aligns with the overall message.
- **Make it easy for your audience to take action:** Provide clear instructions and links to facilitate the desired action.

By mastering the art of storytelling, you can transform your content from mere information into compelling narratives that resonate with your audience, build lasting connections, and inspire action. Remember that storytelling is a skill that can be honed with practice. Experiment with different techniques, analyze your results, and continuously refine your approach to craft narratives that captivate and inspire.

Chapter 6: Crisis Management in Digital Spaces

The digital landscape, while offering immense opportunities, also presents potential pitfalls. A single misstep online can escalate into a full-blown crisis, impacting your reputation and eroding the trust you've worked hard to build. This chapter delves into the crucial aspects of crisis management in the digital realm, equipping you with the knowledge and strategies to navigate challenging situations effectively. We'll cover recognizing a digital crisis, developing a crisis communication plan, managing negative feedback, dealing with trolls and cyberbullying, understanding the role of apologies and transparency, and restoring trust in digital relationships.

Recognizing a Digital Crisis:

A digital crisis can manifest in various forms, from negative social media comments and viral complaints to data breaches and online attacks. Recognizing the early signs of a crisis is crucial for effective intervention.

- **Monitor social media and online mentions:** Use social listening tools to track brand mentions and identify potential issues before they escalate.
- **Pay attention to customer feedback:** Monitor customer reviews, comments, and complaints for recurring themes or negative sentiment.
- **Track website traffic and engagement:** Sudden drops in website traffic or engagement can indicate a potential problem.
- **Be vigilant about security breaches:** Implement robust security measures to protect against data breaches and hacking attempts.

Developing a Crisis Communication Plan:

A well-defined crisis communication plan provides a roadmap for navigating challenging situations effectively. It outlines the steps to be taken, designates roles and responsibilities, and ensures consistent messaging.

- **Identify your crisis management team:** Assemble a team of individuals responsible for handling crisis situations.
- **Establish communication protocols:** Define clear communication channels and procedures for internal and external communication.
- **Develop key messages:** Craft clear and concise messages that address the situation and reassure your audience.
- **Choose appropriate communication channels:** Select the most effective channels for reaching your target audience, such as social media, email, or press releases.

Managing Negative Feedback:

Negative feedback, while often unpleasant, provides valuable insights into areas for improvement. Responding to negative feedback effectively can demonstrate your commitment to customer satisfaction and mitigate potential damage.

- **Respond promptly and professionally:** Acknowledge the feedback and thank the individual for bringing it to your attention.
- **Empathize and apologize:** Express empathy for the individual's experience and apologize for any inconvenience caused.
- **Offer a solution:** Provide a concrete solution to the problem or offer to investigate the matter further.

- **Take the conversation offline:** If the issue is sensitive or requires further discussion, offer to contact the individual directly.

Dealing with Trolls and Cyberbullying:

Trolls and cyberbullies can disrupt online communities and create a hostile environment. Developing strategies for dealing with these individuals is crucial for maintaining a positive online presence.

- **Don't feed the trolls:** Avoid engaging with trolls or responding to their provocations. Ignoring them often diffuses the situation.
- **Report and block:** Report abusive behavior to the platform administrators and block the offending users.
- **Moderate comments:** Implement comment moderation policies to prevent the spread of hate speech and offensive content.
- **Support victims of cyberbullying:** Offer support and encouragement to individuals who have been targeted by cyberbullies.

The Role of Apologies and Transparency:

In the event of a genuine mistake or wrongdoing, a sincere apology and transparent communication can help restore trust and mitigate damage to your reputation.

- **Take responsibility:** Acknowledge your mistake and accept responsibility for your actions.
- **Offer a sincere apology:** Express genuine remorse and apologize for the harm caused.
- **Explain what happened:** Provide a clear and concise explanation of the situation without making excuses.

- **Outline steps for improvement:** Explain what steps you are taking to prevent similar incidents from occurring in the future.

Restoring Trust in Digital Relationships:

Rebuilding trust after a crisis requires consistent positive engagement and a commitment to transparency and open communication.

- **Engage with your audience:** Respond to comments and questions, participate in discussions, and show genuine interest in your community.
- **Be transparent in your communication:** Share updates on the situation and be open about your efforts to address the issue.
- **Deliver on your promises:** Follow through on your commitments and demonstrate your commitment to improvement.

By proactively addressing potential crises, responding to negative feedback effectively, and fostering a culture of transparency and accountability, you can navigate the digital landscape with confidence and build a resilient online presence that can withstand challenges. Remember that crisis management is an ongoing process; continuous monitoring, analysis, and adaptation are crucial for maintaining a positive online reputation and fostering trust with your audience.

Part 3:

Building and Nurturing Online Communities

Chapter 1: Defining Online Communities

The internet has revolutionized human interaction, giving rise to vibrant online communities that transcend geographical boundaries and connect individuals with shared interests. This chapter explores the essence of online communities, delving into their defining characteristics, the importance of shared values, the creation of safe spaces, establishing community guidelines, encouraging member participation, and the crucial role of moderation.

What Constitutes a Digital Community?

A digital community is a group of individuals who interact and connect online, sharing common interests, values, or goals. These communities can exist on various platforms, from social media groups and forums to online gaming platforms and virtual worlds. What distinguishes a digital community from a mere collection of individuals is the sense of belonging, shared identity, and collective purpose.

- **Shared Interest:** Members of a digital community are typically united by a common interest, whether it's a hobby, profession, cause, or shared experience.
- **Interaction and Communication:** Regular interaction and communication between members are essential for fostering a sense of community. This can take various forms, from discussions and comments to shared content and collaborative projects.
- **Shared Identity:** Members often develop a sense of shared identity and belonging, identifying themselves as part of the community.
- **Collective Purpose:** Many digital communities have a collective purpose or goal, such as supporting a cause, sharing knowledge, or providing mutual support.

The Importance of Shared Values:

Shared values form the foundation of a thriving online community. These values guide member behavior, shape the community culture, and foster a sense of belonging. Clearly articulated values create a framework for positive interactions and ensure that the community remains a welcoming and inclusive space.

- **Define core values:** Identify the fundamental principles that guide the community, such as respect, inclusivity, and collaboration.
- **Communicate values clearly:** Make sure the community values are clearly stated and accessible to all members.
- **Reinforce values through moderation:** Enforce community guidelines that uphold the shared values and address violations appropriately.

Creating Safe Spaces Online:

Fostering a safe and inclusive environment is crucial for the health and well-being of any online community. Members should feel comfortable expressing themselves, sharing their thoughts and experiences, and engaging in respectful dialogue without fear of harassment or discrimination.

- **Establish clear guidelines:** Develop community guidelines that outline acceptable behavior and prohibit harassment, discrimination, and other forms of harmful conduct.
- **Empower members to report violations:** Provide clear reporting mechanisms for members to report violations of community guidelines.

- **Moderate content effectively:** Actively moderate content to identify and address violations of community guidelines.
- **Foster a culture of respect:** Encourage members to treat each other with respect and empathy.

Building Community Guidelines:

Community guidelines provide a framework for acceptable behavior within the digital space. These guidelines should be clear, concise, and easily accessible to all members.

- **Address key issues:** Cover topics such as harassment, hate speech, spam, and self-promotion.
- **Use clear and concise language:** Avoid jargon and legalistic language. Make sure the guidelines are easy to understand.
- **Provide examples:** Illustrate acceptable and unacceptable behavior with specific examples.
- **Enforce guidelines consistently:** Apply the guidelines consistently and fairly to all members.

Encouraging Member Participation:

Active participation is the lifeblood of any thriving online community. Encouraging members to contribute their thoughts, ideas, and experiences fosters a sense of belonging and strengthens the community bonds.

- **Create opportunities for interaction:** Organize events, discussions, and challenges that encourage members to participate.
- **Recognize and reward contributions:** Acknowledge and appreciate members who actively contribute to the community.

- **Foster a welcoming and inclusive environment:** Make sure all members feel welcome and comfortable participating.

The Role of Moderation:

Moderation plays a vital role in maintaining a healthy and productive online community. Moderators enforce community guidelines, address conflicts, and ensure that the community remains a safe and welcoming space for all members.

- **Establish clear moderation policies:** Define the roles and responsibilities of moderators.
- **Train moderators effectively:** Provide moderators with the training and resources they need to perform their duties effectively.
- **Be transparent in moderation decisions:** Explain the reasoning behind moderation decisions to maintain trust and accountability.

By understanding the defining characteristics of online communities, fostering shared values, creating safe spaces, establishing clear guidelines, encouraging member participation, and implementing effective moderation strategies, you can cultivate thriving digital communities that provide valuable connections, support, and a sense of belonging for all members. Remember that building a strong online community is an ongoing process; continuous nurturing, adaptation, and engagement are crucial for long-term success.

Chapter 2: Growing Your Community

Building a thriving online community requires more than just establishing a platform; it demands a proactive approach to growth and engagement. This chapter explores the key strategies for expanding your community, attracting new members, nurturing early adopters, incentivizing participation, fostering collaboration, and maintaining quality during the growth process.

Attracting New Members:

Expanding your community begins with attracting new members who share your community's values and interests. This requires a multi-pronged approach, leveraging various channels and tactics to reach your target audience.

- **Promote your community:** Actively promote your community on relevant social media platforms, forums, and websites.
- **Optimize for search engines:** Use relevant keywords and phrases in your community description and content to improve search engine visibility.
- **Run targeted advertising campaigns:** Use social media advertising and other online advertising platforms to reach specific demographics and interests.
- **Partner with other communities:** Collaborate with related communities to cross-promote each other and reach new audiences.
- **Attend online and offline events:** Participate in industry events and meetups to connect with potential members.

Engaging Early Adopters:

Early adopters are the initial members of your community who play a crucial role in shaping its culture and growth. Nurturing these early adopters is essential for building a strong foundation.

- **Recognize and reward early adopters:** Acknowledge and appreciate their contributions to the community. Offer exclusive benefits or recognition for their early support.
- **Solicit feedback and suggestions:** Actively seek input from early adopters to shape the community's development and improve the member experience.
- **Empower early adopters to become community leaders:** Offer opportunities for early adopters to take on leadership roles within the community, such as moderating discussions or organizing events.

Offering Incentives for Joining:

Incentives can motivate potential members to join your community and encourage active participation. These incentives can take various forms, from exclusive content and discounts to early access to new features and opportunities.

- **Offer valuable content:** Provide exclusive content, such as ebooks, webinars, or templates, to members.
- **Provide discounts and special offers:** Offer discounts on products or services to community members.
- **Grant early access to new features:** Give members early access to new features or beta programs.
- **Create a sense of exclusivity:** Offer exclusive access to events, forums, or content.

Collaborative Projects and Initiatives:

Collaborative projects and initiatives provide opportunities for members to connect, share their skills, and contribute to the community. These projects can foster a sense of shared purpose and strengthen community bonds.

- **Organize group projects:** Facilitate group projects, such as creating a community resource guide or organizing a fundraising campaign.
- **Host hackathons and challenges:** Organize hackathons or design challenges to encourage creativity and collaboration.
- **Create collaborative content:** Encourage members to contribute to a shared blog, podcast, or video series.

Building Ambassadors Within Your Community:

Community ambassadors are passionate members who actively promote and advocate for the community. These individuals can play a crucial role in attracting new members and fostering a positive community culture.

- **Identify passionate members:** Recognize members who are actively engaged and enthusiastic about the community.
- **Empower ambassadors to represent the community:** Provide ambassadors with the resources and support they need to promote the community effectively.
- **Recognize and reward ambassadors:** Acknowledge and appreciate the contributions of community ambassadors.

Maintaining Growth Without Sacrificing Quality:

As your community grows, maintaining quality and fostering a positive environment becomes increasingly challenging. Implementing effective moderation strategies and establishing clear community guidelines are essential for preventing spam, harassment, and other negative behaviors.

- **Scale your moderation efforts:** As your community grows, increase your moderation resources to ensure that all content and interactions adhere to community guidelines.
- **Empower members to report violations:** Provide clear reporting mechanisms for members to report violations of community guidelines.
- **Regularly review and update community guidelines:** As your community evolves, review and update your guidelines to reflect the changing needs and expectations of your members.

By implementing these strategies, you can cultivate a thriving online community that attracts new members, fosters engagement, and provides a valuable platform for connection, collaboration, and shared growth. Remember that community growth is an ongoing process; continuous nurturing, adaptation, and a commitment to quality are essential for long-term success.

Chapter 3: Creating Inclusive Communities

Online communities have the power to connect individuals from diverse backgrounds and perspectives, but fostering true inclusivity requires conscious effort and ongoing commitment. This chapter delves into the essential elements of creating inclusive online communities, where every member feels welcome, respected, and valued. We'll explore promoting diversity, eliminating discrimination, creating accessible content, encouraging diverse perspectives, building emotional connections, and addressing exclusion and bias.

Promoting Diversity in Digital Spaces:

Diversity encompasses a wide range of human differences, including race, ethnicity, gender, sexual orientation, age, religion, ability, and socioeconomic status. Promoting diversity within your online community enriches the collective experience, fosters understanding, and creates a more vibrant and representative space.

- **Targeted outreach:** Actively reach out to underrepresented groups and invite them to join your community. Partner with organizations that serve diverse populations.
- **Highlight diverse voices:** Feature content and perspectives from members of different backgrounds. Showcase diverse role models and leaders within the community.
- **Create inclusive events and activities:** Organize events and activities that cater to the interests and needs of diverse members.

Eliminating Discrimination Online:

Discrimination, whether intentional or unintentional, can create a hostile and unwelcoming environment. Implementing clear policies and procedures for addressing discrimination is crucial for maintaining an inclusive community.

- **Establish clear anti-discrimination policies:** Develop and enforce community guidelines that prohibit discrimination based on any protected characteristic.
- **Provide reporting mechanisms:** Offer clear and accessible reporting mechanisms for members to report instances of discrimination.
- **Take swift and decisive action:** Address reports of discrimination promptly and thoroughly. Take appropriate disciplinary action against offenders.
- **Educate members about discrimination:** Provide educational resources and training to raise awareness about different forms of discrimination and promote respectful communication.

Creating Accessible Content:

Accessibility ensures that all members, regardless of their abilities, can access and engage with your community's content. Implementing accessibility best practices creates a more inclusive and equitable experience for everyone.

- **Use alt text for images:** Provide descriptive alt text for all images so that users with visual impairments can understand the content.
- **Caption videos and provide transcripts:** Make video content accessible to users with hearing impairments by providing captions and transcripts.

- **Use clear and concise language:** Avoid jargon and complex language that may be difficult for some users to understand.
- **Design for different devices:** Ensure your community platform and content are accessible on various devices, including desktops, laptops, tablets, and smartphones.

Encouraging Different Perspectives:

A truly inclusive community embraces a diversity of thought and encourages open and respectful dialogue between members with differing viewpoints.

- **Create spaces for respectful disagreement:** Foster an environment where members feel comfortable expressing dissenting opinions without fear of reprisal.
- **Facilitate constructive dialogue:** Encourage members to engage in respectful discussions and debates, even when they disagree.
- **Moderate discussions fairly:** Ensure that all viewpoints are treated with respect and that discussions remain civil and productive.
- **Highlight diverse perspectives:** Showcase content and perspectives from members with different viewpoints to broaden understanding and foster critical thinking.

Building Emotional Connections:

Fostering emotional connections between members strengthens community bonds and creates a sense of belonging. Encourage members to share their experiences, support each other, and celebrate milestones together.

- **Create opportunities for connection:** Organize events and activities that allow members to connect on a personal level.

- **Encourage empathy and understanding:** Foster a culture of empathy and understanding within the community.
- **Celebrate milestones together:** Acknowledge and celebrate members' achievements and milestones.

Addressing Exclusion and Bias:

Exclusion and bias, whether conscious or unconscious, can undermine inclusivity. Addressing these issues requires ongoing vigilance and a commitment to creating a welcoming and equitable environment.

- **Educate members about bias:** Provide educational resources and training to raise awareness about different forms of bias and their impact.
- **Challenge exclusionary behavior:** Address instances of exclusionary behavior promptly and decisively.
- **Promote self-reflection:** Encourage members to reflect on their own biases and how they might be impacting their interactions with others.
- **Foster a culture of accountability:** Hold members accountable for their behavior and create a system for addressing violations of community guidelines.

Creating and maintaining an inclusive online community requires ongoing effort, dedication, and a commitment to continuous improvement. By actively promoting diversity, eliminating discrimination, creating accessible content, encouraging diverse perspectives, building emotional connections, and addressing exclusion and bias, you can cultivate a thriving and welcoming online community where every member feels valued, respected, and empowered to contribute their unique talents and perspectives.

Chapter 4: Sustaining Long-Term Community Engagement

Building a thriving online community is a marathon, not a sprint. Sustaining long-term engagement requires ongoing effort, creativity, and a deep understanding of your community's needs and evolving dynamics. This chapter explores key strategies for keeping members active and involved, fostering a sense of belonging, and nurturing a vibrant and sustainable community over time. We'll cover topics such as organizing virtual events and meetups, recognizing and rewarding loyalty, implementing gamification strategies, building emotional investment, and managing member burnout.

Keeping Members Active and Involved:

Maintaining active participation is crucial for the long-term health of your online community. Creating opportunities for interaction, providing valuable content, and fostering a sense of belonging are essential for keeping members engaged.

- **Regularly publish fresh content:** Keep your community feed active with fresh and engaging content, such as articles, videos, discussions, and polls.
- **Host regular discussions and Q&A sessions:** Facilitate discussions around relevant topics and invite guest speakers to share their expertise.
- **Create challenges and contests:** Organize challenges and contests to encourage friendly competition and boost engagement.
- **Curate user-generated content:** Showcase content created by your community members to foster a sense of ownership and pride.

- **Offer exclusive content and resources:** Provide members with access to exclusive content, resources, and opportunities.

Organizing Virtual Events and Meetups:

Virtual events and meetups provide opportunities for members to connect in real-time, fostering stronger relationships and a sense of community.

- **Host online workshops and webinars:** Offer educational workshops and webinars on topics relevant to your community's interests.
- **Organize virtual conferences and summits:** Bring together experts and community members for larger-scale virtual events.
- **Facilitate online networking events:** Create opportunities for members to connect and network with each other.
- **Host virtual social gatherings:** Organize virtual social events, such as game nights or watch parties, to foster a sense of community and fun.

Recognizing and Rewarding Loyalty:

Recognizing and rewarding loyal community members fosters a sense of appreciation and encourages continued participation.

- **Implement a loyalty program:** Reward active members with badges, points, or exclusive benefits.
- **Recognize member contributions:** Publicly acknowledge and appreciate members who actively contribute to the community.
- **Offer exclusive perks for long-term members:** Provide special perks, such as early access to new

features or discounts on products and services, to long-term members.

Gamification Strategies for Engagement:

Gamification involves incorporating game mechanics, such as points, badges, and leaderboards, to motivate participation and engagement.

- **Award points for contributions:** Award points for activities such as posting, commenting, and sharing content.
- **Create badges and achievements:** Award badges for reaching certain milestones or completing specific challenges.
- **Implement leaderboards:** Create leaderboards to foster friendly competition and recognize top contributors.

Building Emotional Investment:

Creating an emotional connection with your community fosters a sense of belonging and encourages long-term engagement.

- **Share personal stories and experiences:** Connect with your community on a human level by sharing personal stories and experiences.
- **Celebrate milestones together:** Acknowledge and celebrate community milestones, such as anniversaries or membership growth.
- **Support members during challenging times:** Offer support and encouragement to members who are facing difficulties.

Managing Member Burnout:

Burnout can occur when members feel overwhelmed or disengaged from the community. Addressing burnout proactively is crucial for maintaining a healthy and sustainable community.

- **Encourage breaks and time off:** Remind members to take breaks from the community when needed.
- **Provide opportunities for feedback:** Solicit feedback from members to identify potential sources of burnout.
- **Offer support and resources:** Provide members with access to resources and support for managing stress and burnout.
- **Rotate leadership roles:** Distribute responsibilities among different members to prevent burnout among community leaders.

Sustaining long-term community engagement requires ongoing effort, creativity, and a deep understanding of your community's evolving needs. By implementing these strategies, you can cultivate a vibrant and sustainable online community that provides valuable connections, support, and a sense of belonging for years to come. Remember that community building is a continuous journey; adapting to changing dynamics and nurturing relationships are key to long-term success.

Chapter 5: Encouraging Collaborative Creation

Online communities can be powerful engines of creativity and innovation, harnessing the collective intelligence and diverse talents of their members. This chapter explores the strategies and best practices for fostering collaborative creation within your online community, transforming it into a dynamic hub of shared ideas, projects, and achievements. We'll delve into crowdsourcing ideas, facilitating co-creation and partnerships, running digital hackathons and competitions, leveraging user-generated content strategies, establishing collaborative learning spaces, and celebrating member contributions.

Crowdsourcing Ideas from Your Community:

Tapping into the collective intelligence of your community through crowdsourcing can generate a wealth of innovative ideas and solutions.

- **Clearly define the challenge or opportunity:** Provide a clear and concise explanation of the problem you're trying to solve or the opportunity you're exploring.
- **Provide a platform for idea submission:** Create a dedicated space, such as a forum thread, online survey, or dedicated platform, for members to submit their ideas.
- **Encourage diverse perspectives:** Promote participation from members with different backgrounds and expertise.
- **Facilitate discussion and feedback:** Encourage members to discuss and refine each other's ideas.
- **Recognize and reward contributions:** Acknowledge and reward members whose ideas are selected or implemented.

Facilitating Co-creation and Partnerships:

Co-creation involves bringing together community members and external partners to collaborate on projects and initiatives. This can lead to innovative solutions, expand your community's reach, and create valuable partnerships.

- **Identify potential partners:** Seek out organizations or individuals whose values and goals align with your community's mission.
- **Develop clear partnership agreements:** Outline the roles, responsibilities, and expectations of each partner.
- **Create a collaborative workspace:** Provide a shared online space for partners and community members to collaborate on projects.
- **Facilitate communication and coordination:** Ensure clear communication and coordination between all stakeholders.

Running Digital Hackathons and Competitions:

Hackathons and competitions can ignite creativity and innovation within your community, challenging members to develop innovative solutions within a defined timeframe.

- **Define a clear challenge or theme:** Focus the hackathon or competition on a specific problem or area of interest.
- **Provide resources and support:** Offer participants access to resources, mentorship, and technical support.
- **Create a judging criteria:** Establish clear criteria for evaluating submissions.
- **Award prizes and recognition:** Recognize and reward winning teams or individuals.

User-Generated Content Strategies:

User-generated content (UGC) is content created by your community members, such as blog posts, videos, photos, and reviews. Leveraging UGC can enrich your community's content, foster engagement, and build social proof.

- **Encourage UGC creation:** Create opportunities and incentives for members to create and share content.
- **Curate and showcase UGC:** Highlight high-quality UGC on your community platform and social media channels.
- **Recognize and reward content creators:** Acknowledge and reward members who create valuable UGC.

Collaborative Learning Spaces:

Establishing collaborative learning spaces within your community can foster knowledge sharing, skill development, and peer-to-peer learning.

- **Create online courses and workshops:** Offer online courses and workshops on topics relevant to your community's interests.
- **Facilitate study groups and peer mentoring:** Encourage members to form study groups and mentor each other.
- **Develop a knowledge base or resource library:** Create a shared repository of resources, articles, and tutorials.

Celebrating Member Contributions:

Recognizing and celebrating member contributions fosters a sense of appreciation and encourages continued participation.

- **Highlight member achievements:** Showcase member accomplishments, projects, and contributions to the community.
- **Offer public recognition and praise:** Publicly acknowledge and thank members for their contributions.
- **Create a "member spotlight" feature:** Feature individual members and their contributions to the community.

By fostering a culture of collaborative creation, you can transform your online community into a dynamic hub of innovation, shared learning, and collective achievement. Remember that collaboration requires trust, open communication, and a willingness to share ideas and resources. By implementing these strategies and nurturing a supportive environment, you can unlock the full potential of your community and empower its members to achieve remarkable things together.

Chapter 6: Managing Community Dynamics

Online communities, like any social ecosystem, are dynamic and complex. Understanding and effectively managing the intricate interplay of personalities, motivations, and behaviors within your community is crucial for fostering a positive and productive environment. This chapter explores the key strategies for navigating community dynamics, addressing conflicts, fostering positive interactions, and leveraging feedback for continuous improvement. We'll delve into understanding group psychology, handling conflicts, mediation and resolution strategies, encouraging positive interactions, fostering mutual respect, and leveraging feedback for community enhancement.

Understanding Group Psychology:

Understanding the principles of group psychology provides insights into the behavior of individuals within a community setting. This knowledge can help you anticipate potential challenges, manage conflicts effectively, and foster a positive community culture.

- **Social Identity Theory:** Individuals derive part of their identity from the groups they belong to. Fostering a strong sense of community identity can increase member loyalty and engagement. However, it can also lead to in-group bias and exclusionary behavior towards outsiders. Balance fostering a strong community identity with promoting inclusivity and welcoming newcomers.
- **Groupthink:** Groupthink occurs when the desire for harmony within a group overrides critical thinking and independent judgment. Encourage diverse perspectives and create space for healthy disagreement to avoid this

pitfall. Actively solicit dissenting opinions and ensure that all voices are heard.

- **Social Loafing:** In group settings, individuals sometimes exert less effort than they would if working alone. Structure tasks and responsibilities clearly to minimize social loafing and ensure that all members contribute their fair share. Recognize and reward individual contributions to motivate participation.
- **Bystander Effect:** The bystander effect describes the phenomenon where individuals are less likely to intervene in a situation when other people are present. Encourage active participation and empower community members to speak up if they witness harmful behavior.

Handling Conflicts Within Communities:

Conflicts are inevitable in any community. Managing conflicts effectively requires diplomacy, empathy, and a commitment to finding mutually acceptable solutions.

- **Establish clear conflict resolution procedures:** Develop and communicate clear guidelines for addressing conflicts within the community.
- **Encourage direct communication:** Whenever possible, encourage members to communicate directly with each other to resolve conflicts.
- **Mediate when necessary:** If direct communication is unsuccessful, offer mediation services to facilitate a resolution.
- **Take appropriate disciplinary action:** If a member violates community guidelines or engages in harmful behavior, take appropriate disciplinary action, which may include warnings, temporary suspensions, or permanent bans.

Mediation and Resolution Strategies:

Mediation involves a neutral third party facilitating communication and negotiation between conflicting parties. Effective mediation can help resolve conflicts peacefully and restore harmony within the community.

- **Active listening:** Encourage all parties to actively listen to each other's perspectives.
- **Identifying common ground:** Help the parties identify areas of agreement and shared interests.
- **Generating solutions:** Facilitate brainstorming and problem-solving to generate potential solutions.
- **Developing a mutually agreeable agreement:** Guide the parties towards a mutually acceptable agreement that addresses the underlying issues.

Encouraging Positive Interactions:

Fostering a positive and supportive community culture encourages members to engage constructively and build meaningful relationships.

- **Recognize and reward positive behavior:** Acknowledge and appreciate members who contribute positively to the community.
- **Promote acts of kindness and support:** Encourage members to support each other and celebrate each other's successes.
- **Create opportunities for connection:** Organize events and activities that foster connection and build relationships.

Fostering Mutual Respect:

Mutual respect is the cornerstone of a healthy and inclusive community. Encourage members to treat each other with respect, even when they disagree.

- **Promote empathy and understanding:** Encourage members to consider different perspectives and empathize with each other's experiences.
- **Challenge disrespectful behavior:** Address instances of disrespectful behavior promptly and decisively.
- **Model respectful communication:** Set a positive example by communicating respectfully with all members.

Leveraging Feedback for Improvement:

Feedback from community members provides valuable insights for improving the community experience. Regularly solicit feedback and use it to inform your decisions and guide your efforts.

- **Conduct surveys and polls:** Gather feedback through online surveys and polls.
- **Create a feedback forum:** Provide a dedicated space for members to share their feedback and suggestions.
- **Hold regular community meetings:** Organize regular meetings to discuss community issues and gather input from members.
- **Be responsive to feedback:** Demonstrate that you value member feedback by taking action based on their suggestions.

By understanding group dynamics, implementing effective conflict resolution strategies, fostering positive interactions, and leveraging feedback for continuous improvement, you can create a thriving and sustainable online community that provides a valuable platform for connection, collaboration, and shared growth. Remember that managing community dynamics is an ongoing process that requires adaptability, empathy, and a commitment to fostering a positive and inclusive environment.

Part 4:

Digital Branding and Influence

Chapter 1: The Power of Personal Branding

In today's digital age, personal branding is no longer a luxury; it's a necessity. It's the process of defining and communicating your unique value proposition to the world, establishing yourself as a recognizable and respected figure in your field. This chapter explores the essential elements of crafting a compelling personal brand, covering topics such as defining your brand identity, building consistency across platforms, telling your story authentically, leveraging personal branding for career advancement, defining your unique selling proposition, and growing your professional network.

Crafting Your Brand Identity:

Your brand identity is the essence of who you are and what you represent. It encompasses your values, skills, experience, and personality. Defining your brand identity is the first step in building a strong personal brand.

- **Identify your strengths and passions:** What are you good at? What do you enjoy doing? What are you passionate about?
- **Define your target audience:** Who are you trying to reach with your personal brand? What are their needs and interests?
- **Develop a brand statement:** Craft a concise statement that summarizes your brand identity and value proposition.
- **Choose a visual identity:** Select colors, fonts, and imagery that reflect your brand personality.

Building Consistency Across Platforms:

Maintaining consistency across your online presence is crucial for building a recognizable and trustworthy brand. This includes using consistent profile pictures, usernames, bios, and messaging across different platforms.

- **Use a professional headshot:** Your profile picture should be a professional headshot that reflects your brand identity.
- **Craft a compelling bio:** Your bio should summarize your expertise and experience in a concise and engaging manner.
- **Use consistent branding elements:** Use the same colors, fonts, and imagery across all your online platforms.
- **Maintain a consistent tone of voice:** Communicate in a way that is authentic and consistent with your brand personality.

Telling Your Story Authentically:

Sharing your personal story in an authentic and engaging way can create a deeper connection with your audience and differentiate you from the competition.

- **Be genuine and transparent:** Share your experiences, challenges, and triumphs honestly.
- **Focus on your values:** Communicate your core values and beliefs through your story.
- **Highlight your unique perspective:** What makes your story different? What unique insights can you offer?
- **Use storytelling techniques:** Employ storytelling techniques, such as narrative structure, character development, and emotional appeal, to make your story more compelling.

Personal Branding for Career Advancement:

A strong personal brand can be a powerful asset in your career development, opening doors to new opportunities and positioning you as a leader in your field.

- **Showcase your expertise:** Use your online presence to demonstrate your skills and knowledge.
- **Build your network:** Connect with other professionals in your industry and build relationships.
- **Position yourself as a thought leader:** Share your insights and perspectives on industry trends and challenges.
- **Attract recruiters and potential employers:** A strong online presence can attract the attention of recruiters and potential employers.

Defining Your Unique Selling Proposition (USP):

Your USP is what sets you apart from the competition. It's the unique value you offer that others don't. Defining your USP is crucial for attracting your target audience and establishing yourself as a valuable resource.

- **Identify your unique skills and talents:** What are you exceptionally good at? What skills do you possess that are in high demand?
- **Analyze your competition:** What do your competitors offer? How can you differentiate yourself?
- **Focus on the benefits you offer:** How can your skills and talents benefit your target audience? What problems can you solve for them?
- **Craft a concise and compelling USP statement:** Summarize your USP in a clear and concise statement that resonates with your target audience.

Growing Your Professional Network:

Building a strong professional network is essential for career advancement and personal growth. Your online presence can be a powerful tool for connecting with other professionals and expanding your network.

- **Connect on LinkedIn:** LinkedIn is the leading platform for professional networking. Build a strong profile and connect with other professionals in your field.
- **Engage in online communities:** Participate in online forums, groups, and discussions related to your industry.
- **Attend virtual events and webinars:** Networking events and webinars offer opportunities to connect with other professionals and learn new skills.
- **Follow industry leaders and influencers:** Stay up-to-date on industry trends and connect with influential figures in your field.

By crafting a compelling personal brand, telling your story authentically, leveraging your online presence for career advancement, defining your unique selling proposition, and growing your professional network, you can establish yourself as a respected figure in your field and unlock new opportunities for personal and professional growth. Remember that personal branding is an ongoing process; continuously refining your brand, adapting to changing trends, and nurturing relationships are crucial for long-term success.

Chapter 2: Social Media Influence and Trust

In the digital age, social media has become a powerful platform for building influence and shaping public opinion. However, with this power comes responsibility. This chapter explores the dynamics of social media influence, emphasizing the importance of building trust, maintaining authenticity, and engaging responsibly with your audience. We'll delve into building credibility in digital spaces, the importance of transparency and authenticity, strategies for engaging with followers and building trust, understanding the psychology of influence, analyzing case studies of successful influencers, and leveraging social proof for growth.

Building Credibility in Digital Spaces:

Credibility is the foundation of influence. Building credibility in the digital realm requires consistent effort, demonstrated expertise, and authentic engagement.

- **Share valuable content:** Provide your audience with informative, insightful, and entertaining content that demonstrates your knowledge and expertise.
- **Engage in meaningful conversations:** Participate in discussions, respond to comments and questions, and build relationships with your followers.
- **Be transparent and authentic:** Share your experiences, perspectives, and values honestly. Avoid portraying a false or idealized image of yourself.
- **Build a strong reputation:** Maintain a positive online reputation by adhering to ethical principles and avoiding controversial or offensive behavior.

Transparency and Authenticity in Influence:

Transparency and authenticity are crucial for building trust with your audience. Be genuine in your interactions, share your experiences honestly, and avoid misleading or deceptive practices.

- **Disclose sponsored content:** Clearly label any sponsored content or paid partnerships to maintain transparency with your audience.
- **Be upfront about your motivations:** What are your goals for building influence? Be honest with your audience about your intentions.
- **Share your struggles and challenges:** Don't be afraid to show your vulnerability and share your challenges. This can make you more relatable and build trust with your audience.

Engaging with Followers and Building Trust:

Building a loyal following requires active engagement and genuine interaction with your audience. Respond to comments and messages, participate in discussions, and create opportunities for two-way communication.

- **Ask questions and solicit feedback:** Encourage your audience to share their thoughts and opinions. Use their feedback to improve your content and engagement strategies.
- **Run polls and surveys:** Engage your audience with interactive content, such as polls and surveys.
- **Host live Q&A sessions:** Connect with your audience in real-time through live Q&A sessions.
- **Create a sense of community:** Foster a sense of belonging by encouraging interaction and creating opportunities for members to connect with each other.

The Psychology of Influence:

Understanding the psychological principles that underpin influence can help you craft more effective communication strategies.

- **Social Proof:** People are more likely to follow the lead of others, especially those they perceive as credible or influential. Leverage social proof by showcasing testimonials, endorsements, and social media shares.
- **Authority:** People tend to defer to authority figures. Establish your expertise and credibility to build authority within your niche.
- **Scarcity:** People value things that are scarce or limited. Create a sense of urgency or exclusivity around your content or offerings.
- **Reciprocity:** People feel obligated to reciprocate when they receive something of value. Offer valuable content and resources to your audience to build reciprocity.

Case Studies of Successful Influencers:

Analyzing case studies of successful influencers can provide valuable insights into effective strategies and best practices.

- **Identify influencers in your niche:** Research successful influencers who are operating in your industry or area of interest.
- **Analyze their strategies:** Study their content, engagement tactics, and audience building strategies.
- **Identify key success factors:** What factors have contributed to their success? What lessons can you learn from their experience?

Leveraging Social Proof for Growth:

Social proof is a powerful tool for building trust and credibility, which can lead to increased followers and engagement.

- **Showcase testimonials and reviews:** Feature positive testimonials and reviews from satisfied customers or clients.
- **Display social media share counts:** Show the number of times your content has been shared on social media.
- **Highlight media mentions and awards:** Showcase any media mentions or awards you have received.
- **Partner with other influencers:** Collaborating with other influencers can expose you to a wider audience and build social proof.

By focusing on building credibility, maintaining transparency and authenticity, engaging actively with your audience, understanding the psychology of influence, learning from successful influencers, and leveraging social proof, you can cultivate a strong and positive influence on social media. Remember that building genuine influence takes time and effort. Focus on providing value to your audience, building authentic relationships, and engaging responsibly in the digital space.

Chapter 3: Collaborations and Partnerships

In the interconnected digital landscape, collaborations and partnerships offer powerful avenues for expanding your reach, accessing new audiences, and achieving shared goals. This chapter explores the strategic advantages of collaborations and partnerships, providing a framework for identifying potential collaborators, structuring mutually beneficial agreements, and measuring the success of collaborative endeavors. We'll delve into strategic collaborations for growth, navigating cross-industry partnerships, exploring joint ventures and co-creation opportunities, building win-win relationships, understanding influencer marketing and affiliate programs, and measuring the success of collaborations.

Strategic Collaborations for Growth:

Strategic collaborations can fuel growth by leveraging the strengths and resources of multiple parties. Identifying synergistic partnerships that align with your goals and target audience is crucial for maximizing the impact of collaborative efforts.

- **Identify potential collaborators:** Research individuals, businesses, or organizations whose values, audience, and expertise complement your own. Look for opportunities to create mutually beneficial partnerships.
- **Define shared goals and objectives:** Clearly outline the goals you hope to achieve through the collaboration. Ensure that all parties are aligned on the desired outcomes.
- **Develop a collaborative strategy:** Outline the specific actions, timelines, and responsibilities of each partner. Establish clear communication channels and reporting mechanisms.

Cross-Industry Partnerships:

Venturing beyond your immediate industry can unlock new opportunities and expose your brand to a wider audience. Cross-industry partnerships can be particularly effective for reaching new customer segments and expanding your market reach.

- **Identify complementary industries:** Explore industries that align with your target audience's interests or needs. For example, a fitness brand might partner with a healthy food company.
- **Find common ground:** Identify shared values or goals that can form the basis of a mutually beneficial partnership.
- **Develop creative co-marketing campaigns:** Explore innovative ways to collaborate on marketing campaigns, such as joint social media promotions, cross-promotional email campaigns, or co-branded events.

Joint Ventures and Co-creation:

Joint ventures involve creating a new entity or product together, while co-creation focuses on developing content or experiences collaboratively. Both approaches can lead to innovative outcomes and strengthen relationships between partners.

- **Joint Ventures:** Define the ownership structure, responsibilities, and profit-sharing arrangements clearly. Develop a comprehensive business plan for the joint venture.
- **Co-creation:** Establish a shared creative vision and define the roles and contributions of each partner. Create a collaborative workspace where partners can share ideas, feedback, and resources.

Building Win-Win Relationships:

Successful collaborations are built on mutually beneficial relationships where all parties derive value from the partnership. Focus on creating win-win scenarios that benefit everyone involved.

- **Open communication:** Maintain open and honest communication throughout the collaboration process. Address any challenges or concerns promptly and constructively.
- **Mutual respect:** Treat your partners with respect and value their contributions.
- **Flexibility and compromise:** Be willing to compromise and adapt to changing circumstances.

Influencer Marketing and Affiliate Programs:

Influencer marketing involves partnering with individuals who have a significant following and influence within your target audience. Affiliate programs incentivize partners to promote your products or services in exchange for a commission.

- **Influencer Marketing:** Carefully select influencers whose values and audience align with your brand. Develop clear campaign objectives and measurement metrics. Disclose sponsored content transparently.
- **Affiliate Programs:** Offer competitive commission rates and provide affiliates with the resources they need to promote your offerings effectively. Track affiliate performance and reward top performers.

Measuring the Success of Collaborations:

Measuring the impact of your collaborations is crucial for assessing their effectiveness and optimizing future partnerships. Establish clear metrics and track your progress throughout the collaboration.

- **Define key performance indicators (KPIs):** Identify the metrics that will be used to measure the success of the collaboration, such as reach, engagement, website traffic, or sales.
- **Track your results:** Monitor your progress against the defined KPIs throughout the collaboration.
- **Analyze your findings:** Evaluate the results of the collaboration and identify areas for improvement. Use your findings to inform future partnerships and optimize your collaborative strategies.

By strategically selecting collaborators, developing mutually beneficial agreements, and measuring the success of your efforts, you can leverage the power of collaborations and partnerships to expand your reach, enhance your brand reputation, and achieve shared goals. Remember that collaboration is an ongoing process; nurturing relationships, adapting to changing circumstances, and maintaining open communication are crucial for long-term success.

Chapter 4: Monetizing Your Digital Presence

Building a strong digital presence takes time and effort. Monetizing that presence effectively requires a strategic approach that aligns with your audience, brand, and overall goals. This chapter explores various avenues for generating revenue from your digital platforms, covering topics such as turning followers into customers, creating and selling digital products, monetizing through sponsored content, offering consulting and coaching services, leveraging affiliate marketing, and establishing membership models.

Turning Followers into Customers:

Cultivating a loyal following is the first step towards monetization. Converting followers into paying customers requires building trust, providing value, and offering products or services that meet their needs.

- **Understand your audience:** What are their pain points? What solutions are they seeking? What are their purchasing habits?
- **Build relationships:** Engage with your followers, respond to comments and messages, and foster a sense of community.
- **Provide valuable content:** Offer informative, entertaining, and engaging content that demonstrates your expertise and builds trust.
- **Promote your offerings strategically:** Promote your products or services in a way that feels natural and authentic. Avoid being overly promotional or pushy.

Creating and Selling Digital Products:

Digital products, such as ebooks, online courses, templates, and software, offer a scalable and cost-effective way to monetize your digital presence.

- **Identify a market need:** What problems can you solve for your audience? What knowledge or skills can you share?
- **Create high-quality products:** Invest time and effort in creating valuable and well-designed products that meet your audience's needs.
- **Choose appropriate pricing:** Research market prices for similar products and set a price that reflects the value you offer.
- **Market your products effectively:** Promote your digital products through your website, social media channels, email marketing, and other online platforms.

Monetizing Through Sponsored Content:

Sponsored content involves partnering with brands to create content that promotes their products or services. This can be a lucrative way to monetize your digital presence, but it's crucial to maintain transparency and authenticity.

- **Disclose sponsored content clearly:** Always disclose sponsored content to your audience to maintain trust and transparency.
- **Partner with brands that align with your values:** Choose brands that are relevant to your audience and align with your personal brand.
- **Create high-quality content:** Ensure that sponsored content is valuable and engaging for your audience. Avoid being overly promotional or pushy.

Offering Consulting and Coaching Services:

If you have expertise in a particular area, offering consulting or coaching services can be a valuable way to monetize your knowledge and skills.

- **Define your niche:** What specific area of expertise do you offer? What problems can you solve for your clients?
- **Develop a service offering:** Clearly outline your services, pricing, and target audience.
- **Market your services effectively:** Promote your consulting or coaching services through your website, social media channels, and networking.

Leveraging Affiliate Marketing:

Affiliate marketing involves promoting other companies' products or services and earning a commission on each sale. This can be a passive income stream, but it requires careful selection of affiliate partners and strategic promotion.

- **Choose reputable affiliate programs:** Partner with companies that offer high-quality products or services and have a good reputation.
- **Promote products that are relevant to your audience:** Only promote products that you believe will be valuable to your followers.
- **Disclose affiliate links transparently:** Always disclose affiliate links to your audience to maintain transparency and trust.

Creating a Membership Model:

Membership models offer exclusive content and benefits to paying subscribers. This can create a recurring revenue stream and foster a sense of community among your most loyal followers.

- **Define your membership tiers:** Offer different membership levels with varying benefits and pricing.
- **Provide exclusive content and resources:** Offer members access to exclusive content, such as online courses, webinars, or community forums.
- **Build a community:** Foster a sense of community among your members through exclusive events and online interactions.

Monetizing your digital presence requires a strategic approach that aligns with your audience, brand, and overall goals. By exploring these diverse avenues for generating revenue, you can transform your digital platform into a sustainable business and achieve financial success while providing value to your audience. Remember that building trust and maintaining authenticity are paramount for long-term monetization success. Focus on creating valuable content, building strong relationships with your audience, and promoting your offerings in a way that feels natural and authentic.

Chapter 5: The Ethics of Digital Influence

The rise of digital influence brings with it a set of ethical considerations that must be carefully navigated. As individuals gain influence online, they have a responsibility to wield that influence responsibly and ethically. This chapter explores the ethical implications of digital influence, covering topics such as maintaining integrity, navigating conflicts of interest, disclosing sponsored content, being honest in brand deals, dealing with backlash from misleading content, and understanding legal considerations.

Understanding the Ethical Implications:

Digital influence can shape opinions, behaviors, and purchasing decisions. Influencers have a responsibility to their audience to be truthful, transparent, and ethical in their online activities.

- **Honesty and Integrity:** Maintain honesty and integrity in all your online interactions. Avoid misleading or deceptive practices.
- **Respect for your audience:** Treat your audience with respect and value their trust. Avoid exploiting their vulnerabilities or manipulating their emotions.
- **Responsibility for your content:** Take responsibility for the content you create and share. Ensure that it is accurate, factual, and does not promote harmful stereotypes or misinformation.
- **Social impact:** Consider the potential impact of your content on society. Avoid promoting harmful products or behaviors.

Maintaining Integrity in Digital Promotion:

Promoting products or services online requires maintaining integrity and transparency. Avoid making false or misleading claims, and always disclose any sponsored content or paid partnerships.

- **Truthful advertising:** Ensure that your promotional content is truthful and accurate. Avoid exaggerating or misrepresenting the benefits of a product or service.
- **Transparency with sponsorships:** Clearly disclose any sponsored content or paid partnerships to your audience. Use clear and concise language, such as #sponsored or #ad.
- **Authentic endorsements:** Only endorse products or services that you genuinely believe in and use yourself. Avoid promoting products that you have not personally tried or that do not align with your values.

Navigating Conflicts of Interest:

Conflicts of interest can arise when an influencer's personal interests conflict with their professional obligations. Disclose any potential conflicts of interest to your audience and take steps to mitigate their impact.

- **Transparency with potential conflicts:** Be transparent with your audience about any potential conflicts of interest. For example, if you are promoting a product from a company that you have a financial stake in, disclose this information.
- **Prioritizing audience interests:** Always prioritize the interests of your audience over your own personal gain.
- **Recusal from endorsements:** If a conflict of interest cannot be mitigated, recuse yourself from endorsing the product or service in question.

Honesty in Brand Deals:

Brand deals and partnerships offer valuable opportunities for influencers, but it's crucial to maintain honesty and transparency in these collaborations.

- **Due diligence with brand partners:** Thoroughly research potential brand partners to ensure that they align with your values and that their products or services are of high quality.
- **Authentic brand alignment:** Only partner with brands that you genuinely believe in and that are relevant to your audience.
- **Clear contractual agreements:** Establish clear contractual agreements with brand partners that outline the scope of the collaboration, payment terms, and other important details.

Dealing with Backlash from Misleading Content:

Even with the best intentions, mistakes can happen. If you face backlash from misleading content, take swift and decisive action to address the situation.

- **Acknowledge the mistake:** Admit your mistake and take responsibility for your actions.
- **Apologize sincerely:** Offer a sincere apology to your audience for any harm caused.
- **Correct the misinformation:** Provide accurate information and correct any misleading statements.
- **Learn from the experience:** Take steps to prevent similar incidents from occurring in the future.

Legal Considerations in Digital Influence:

Digital influence is subject to various legal regulations, such as advertising disclosure requirements and consumer protection laws. Familiarize yourself with the relevant legal frameworks and ensure that your activities comply with applicable laws.

- **Advertising disclosures:** Familiarize yourself with the advertising disclosure guidelines established by the Federal Trade Commission (FTC) and other regulatory bodies.
- **Copyright and intellectual property:** Respect copyright laws and intellectual property rights. Obtain permission before using copyrighted material.
- **Data privacy and security:** Protect the privacy and security of your audience's data. Comply with data privacy regulations, such as GDPR and CCPA.

By understanding and adhering to ethical principles, maintaining transparency, navigating conflicts of interest responsibly, being honest in brand deals, addressing backlash effectively, and complying with legal regulations, you can build a sustainable and impactful digital influence that benefits both you and your audience. Remember that ethical conduct is not a one-time event; it's an ongoing commitment that requires constant vigilance and self-reflection.

Chapter 6: Scaling Your Online Presence

Growing your online presence from a modest following to a wider audience requires a strategic approach that encompasses content creation, platform expansion, audience engagement, and team building. This chapter explores the key strategies for scaling your digital footprint, expanding your reach, and maximizing your impact. We'll delve into expanding beyond social media platforms, building a website or blog, launching a podcast or video channel, scaling content production, delegating and building a team, and developing a long-term vision for growth.

Expanding Beyond Social Media Platforms:

While social media platforms provide a valuable foundation, diversifying your online presence beyond these platforms is crucial for long-term sustainability and growth.

- **Building a Website or Blog:** A website or blog serves as a central hub for your online presence, providing a platform to showcase your expertise, share your story, and offer valuable content. This allows you to own your content and control the user experience. Optimize your website for search engines (SEO) to attract organic traffic.
- **Email Marketing:** Building an email list allows you to communicate directly with your audience, nurture leads, and promote your offerings. Offer valuable incentives, such as free ebooks or exclusive content, to encourage sign-ups. Segment your list to personalize your messaging and target specific audience segments.

Launching a Podcast or Video Channel:

Podcasts and video channels offer engaging formats for connecting with your audience, sharing your expertise, and building a loyal following.

- **Podcast:** Choose a niche topic that aligns with your expertise and target audience. Invest in quality recording equipment and editing software. Promote your podcast through social media, email marketing, and podcast directories.
- **Video Channel:** Create high-quality videos that are informative, entertaining, or inspiring. Optimize your videos for search engines (SEO) and promote them across your social media channels. Engage with viewers in the comments section.

Scaling Content Production:

As your audience grows, scaling your content production becomes essential for maintaining engagement and meeting the increasing demand for content.

- **Content Calendar:** Develop a content calendar to plan and schedule your content in advance. This helps maintain consistency and ensures a diverse mix of topics.
- **Repurposing Content:** Repurpose existing content into different formats. For example, a blog post can be turned into a video, infographic, or series of social media updates.
- **Content Batching:** Create multiple pieces of content in one dedicated session. This improves efficiency and allows you to focus on content creation without distractions.

Delegating and Building a Team:

As your online presence expands, delegating tasks and building a team becomes essential for managing your workload and maintaining quality.

- **Identify tasks to delegate:** Determine which tasks can be delegated to others, such as social media management, content creation, or graphic design.
- **Hire freelancers or virtual assistants:** Utilize freelance platforms or virtual assistant services to find skilled professionals to assist you.
- **Build a team:** As your needs grow, consider building a dedicated team to manage different aspects of your online presence. Clearly define roles and responsibilities.

Long-Term Vision and Growth Strategies:

Developing a long-term vision for your online presence provides direction and helps you stay focused on your goals. Regularly review and adapt your strategies to stay ahead of the curve and capitalize on emerging opportunities.

- **Set long-term goals:** Where do you see your online presence in five years? Ten years? Set ambitious yet achievable goals.
- **Develop a growth strategy:** Outline the specific steps you will take to achieve your long-term goals. This may include expanding into new platforms, developing new products or services, or building strategic partnerships.
- **Stay adaptable:** The digital landscape is constantly evolving. Be prepared to adapt your strategies and embrace new technologies.
- **Monitor your progress:** Track your progress against your goals and make adjustments as needed.

Continuously analyze data and adapt your approach based on your findings.

Scaling your online presence requires a strategic blend of content creation, platform expansion, audience engagement, and team building. By implementing these strategies, you can expand your reach, maximize your impact, and achieve your long-term goals in the digital landscape. Remember that growth is an ongoing journey; continuous learning, adaptation, and a commitment to providing value to your audience are essential for sustained success.

Part 5:

Advanced Strategies for Building Digital Social Connections

Chapter 1: Leveraging Data for Social Success

In the digital age, data is the lifeblood of informed decision-making. Understanding how to collect, analyze, and interpret data related to your online presence is crucial for optimizing your strategies, maximizing your reach, and achieving your goals. This chapter explores the power of data-driven decision-making in the context of building a successful online presence. We'll cover collecting and analyzing data, using insights to shape strategies, understanding consumer behavior, predicting trends with data, segmenting audiences for personalization, and using A/B testing for optimization.

Collecting and Analyzing Data:

Collecting relevant data is the first step in data-driven decision-making. Various tools and platforms provide access to a wealth of data about your audience, content performance, and online activity.

- **Website analytics:** Tools like Google Analytics provide data on website traffic, user behavior, demographics, and conversion rates. This data can be used to understand how users interact with your website, identify areas for improvement, and track the effectiveness of your content marketing efforts.
- **Social media analytics:** Each social media platform offers its own analytics dashboard, providing insights into audience demographics, engagement metrics, content performance, and follower growth. Use this data to understand your audience, tailor your content, and optimize your social media strategies.
- **Social listening tools:** Social listening tools track mentions of your brand, competitors, and industry keywords across social media and other online platforms. This data can provide valuable insights into

brand sentiment, identify potential crises, and inform your content strategy.

Using Insights to Shape Strategies:

Data analysis provides valuable insights into audience behavior, content performance, and market trends. Use these insights to inform your strategies and make data-driven decisions.

- **Content Strategy:** Analyze data on content performance to understand what resonates with your audience. Identify high-performing content formats, topics, and distribution channels. Use this data to refine your content strategy and create more engaging content.
- **Audience Engagement:** Analyze data on audience demographics, interests, and online behavior to tailor your engagement strategies. Personalize your messaging, target specific audience segments, and create content that resonates with their needs and interests.
- **Platform Optimization:** Analyze data on platform performance to identify which platforms are most effective for reaching your target audience. Focus your efforts on the platforms that generate the highest engagement and ROI.

Understanding Consumer Behavior:

Data analysis can reveal valuable insights into consumer behavior, helping you understand their motivations, preferences, and purchasing decisions.

- **Purchase patterns:** Analyze data on purchasing behavior to understand what motivates consumers to buy. Identify key factors that influence their decisions, such as price, product features, or brand reputation.

- **Content consumption habits:** Analyze data on content consumption to understand what type of content resonates with your audience. Identify preferred content formats, topics, and distribution channels.
- **Online behavior:** Analyze data on online behavior, such as website browsing history and social media activity, to understand how consumers interact with your brand online.

Predicting Trends with Data:

Analyzing historical data and identifying emerging patterns can help you predict future trends and adapt your strategies proactively.

- **Trend analysis:** Use data analysis tools to identify emerging trends in your industry or niche. Stay ahead of the curve by adapting your content and marketing strategies to capitalize on these trends.
- **Predictive modeling:** Use statistical models to predict future outcomes based on historical data. This can help you make informed decisions about resource allocation, product development, and marketing campaigns.

Segmenting Audiences for Personalization:

Segmenting your audience into distinct groups based on shared characteristics, such as demographics, interests, or behavior, allows you to personalize your messaging and tailor your content to their specific needs.

- **Demographic segmentation:** Segment your audience based on factors such as age, gender, location, education, and income.
- **Behavioral segmentation:** Segment your audience based on their online behavior, such as website

browsing history, purchase history, and social media activity.

- **Psychographic segmentation:** Segment your audience based on their values, interests, and lifestyle.

Using A/B Testing for Optimization:

A/B testing involves comparing two versions of a webpage, advertisement, or other marketing asset to determine which performs better. This data-driven approach allows you to optimize your campaigns and improve your results.

- **Define your testing variables:** Identify the specific elements you want to test, such as headlines, images, call-to-action buttons, or layout.
- **Create two versions:** Create two versions of your asset, each with a different variation of the testing variable.
- **Run the test:** Show each version to a segment of your audience and track their behavior.
- **Analyze the results:** Determine which version performed better based on your chosen metrics, such as click-through rate or conversion rate.

By leveraging data effectively, you can gain valuable insights into your audience, optimize your strategies, and achieve greater success in the digital landscape. Data-driven decision-making empowers you to make informed choices, allocate resources effectively, and adapt to the ever-evolving online environment. Remember that data analysis is an ongoing process. Continuously collect, analyze, and interpret data to refine your approach and maximize your impact.

Chapter 2: Navigating the Digital Algorithm

The digital landscape is governed by complex algorithms that determine what content users see and how they interact with online platforms. Understanding these algorithms is crucial for maximizing your reach, engagement, and overall impact. This chapter explores the intricacies of digital algorithms, offering strategies for optimizing your content and navigating the ever-evolving online environment. We'll delve into understanding social media algorithms, optimizing for maximum reach, exploring the role of paid advertising, adapting to algorithm changes, creating shareable content, and engaging strategically with the algorithm.

Understanding Social Media Algorithms:

Each social media platform employs its own unique algorithm, a complex set of rules and calculations that determines which content is shown to users and in what order. While the specifics of each algorithm are often kept confidential, understanding the general principles can help you optimize your content for greater visibility.

- **Relevance:** Algorithms prioritize content that is relevant to the user's interests, past behavior, and social connections.
- **Engagement:** Content that generates high levels of engagement, such as likes, comments, shares, and saves, is more likely to be shown to a wider audience.
- **Timeliness:** Recent content is often prioritized over older content. Posting consistently and at optimal times can improve visibility.
- **Content Quality:** Algorithms favor high-quality content that is informative, entertaining, or valuable to the user.

Optimizing for Maximum Reach:

Reaching a wider audience organically requires understanding the factors that influence algorithmic visibility and tailoring your content accordingly.

- **Keyword Research:** Identify relevant keywords and phrases that your target audience is searching for. Incorporate these keywords into your content, captions, and hashtags.
- **Hashtag Strategy:** Use relevant hashtags to increase the discoverability of your content. Research popular and niche hashtags related to your topic.
- **Content Format:** Experiment with different content formats, such as videos, images, carousels, and stories, to see what resonates best with your audience and the algorithm.
- **Posting Schedule:** Analyze your audience's online behavior to determine the optimal times to post. Consistency is key for maintaining visibility.

The Role of Paid Advertising:

Paid advertising can amplify your reach and target specific audience segments. While organic reach is valuable, paid advertising can supplement your efforts and accelerate growth.

- **Targeted Advertising:** Social media advertising platforms allow you to target specific demographics, interests, and behaviors. This ensures that your ads are seen by the most relevant audience.
- **Ad Formats:** Experiment with different ad formats, such as image ads, video ads, and sponsored posts, to see what performs best.

- **Budgeting and Bidding:** Set a budget for your advertising campaigns and experiment with different bidding strategies to optimize your spending.
- **Performance Tracking:** Monitor the performance of your ads closely and make adjustments based on the data.

Algorithm Changes and Adaptation:

Social media algorithms are constantly evolving. Staying informed about algorithm updates and adapting your strategies accordingly is crucial for maintaining visibility.

- **Follow industry news:** Stay updated on the latest news and announcements from social media platforms.
- **Analyze your data:** Monitor your reach and engagement metrics closely to identify any changes in performance that may be attributed to algorithm updates.
- **Experiment and adapt:** Be willing to experiment with different strategies and adapt your approach as needed.

Creating Shareable Content:

Content that is valuable, entertaining, or informative is more likely to be shared by your audience, expanding your reach organically.

- **High-Quality Visuals:** Use eye-catching images and videos to capture attention.
- **Compelling Storytelling:** Craft narratives that resonate with your audience's emotions and values.
- **Practical Tips and Advice:** Share helpful tips and advice that your audience can apply to their own lives.
- **Interactive Content:** Engage your audience with polls, quizzes, and other interactive content formats.

Engaging with the Algorithm:

Understanding how the algorithm interprets user behavior can help you optimize your engagement strategies.

- **Encourage interaction:** Ask questions, respond to comments, and encourage your audience to engage with your content.
- **Community Building:** Foster a sense of community by encouraging interaction between your followers.
- **Respond to comments and messages promptly:** Show your audience that you value their engagement by responding to their comments and messages in a timely manner.

By understanding the dynamics of digital algorithms, optimizing your content for maximum reach, utilizing paid advertising strategically, adapting to algorithm changes, creating shareable content, and engaging actively with your audience, you can navigate the complexities of the digital landscape and achieve greater visibility and impact. Remember that algorithm optimization is an ongoing process; continuous learning, experimentation, and adaptation are crucial for staying ahead of the curve.

Chapter 3: The Role of Artificial Intelligence in Social Connection

Artificial intelligence (AI) is rapidly transforming the digital landscape, including how we connect, communicate, and build relationships online. This chapter explores the growing role of AI in social connection, examining its applications, benefits, and potential challenges. We'll delve into AI tools for content creation, personalization through AI, leveraging AI for audience insights, utilizing chatbots for customer interaction, automating engagement with AI, and addressing the ethical concerns surrounding AI in digital spaces.

AI Tools for Content Creation:

AI-powered tools are revolutionizing content creation, offering new possibilities for generating, optimizing, and distributing content.

- **AI Writing Assistants:** These tools can assist with generating various types of content, from blog posts and articles to social media captions and email marketing copy. They can help overcome writer's block, improve grammar and style, and even suggest relevant topics.
- **AI Image Generators:** AI can generate unique images based on text prompts, providing visually appealing content for social media, websites, and marketing materials.
- **AI Video Editing Tools:** AI-powered video editing tools can automate tasks such as transcription, subtitling, and even video generation, freeing up content creators to focus on creative aspects.

Personalization Through AI:

AI enables personalized experiences online, tailoring content, recommendations, and interactions to individual user preferences.

- **Personalized Content Recommendations:** AI algorithms analyze user data, such as browsing history, past purchases, and social media activity, to recommend relevant content. This enhances user experience and increases engagement.
- **Targeted Advertising:** AI powers targeted advertising campaigns, ensuring that ads are seen by the most relevant audience segments. This improves ad effectiveness and reduces wasted ad spend.
- **Personalized Product Recommendations:** E-commerce platforms utilize AI to recommend products based on user preferences, purchase history, and browsing behavior.

AI for Audience Insights:

AI can analyze vast amounts of data to provide valuable insights into audience demographics, interests, behavior, and sentiment.

- **Social Listening:** AI-powered social listening tools can analyze social media conversations, online reviews, and other online mentions to understand audience sentiment towards your brand, products, or competitors.
- **Predictive Analytics:** AI can predict future trends and behaviors based on historical data, allowing you to anticipate audience needs and adapt your strategies proactively.

- **Sentiment Analysis:** AI can analyze text data to determine the emotional tone of online conversations, providing insights into audience sentiment and potential PR crises.

Chatbots for Customer Interaction:

AI-powered chatbots provide automated customer support, answering frequently asked questions, resolving simple issues, and guiding customers through online processes.

- **24/7 Availability:** Chatbots provide round-the-clock support, improving customer satisfaction and reducing response times.
- **Personalized Interactions:** AI chatbots can personalize interactions based on user data, providing tailored recommendations and support.
- **Lead Generation:** Chatbots can be used to qualify leads and collect customer information.

Automating Engagement with AI:

AI can automate various engagement tasks, freeing up time for content creators and community managers to focus on more strategic activities.

- **Social Media Scheduling:** AI-powered tools can schedule social media posts at optimal times, maximizing reach and engagement.
- **Automated Responses:** AI can generate automated responses to common inquiries on social media and other platforms.
- **Content Curation:** AI can curate relevant content from various sources, providing valuable resources to your audience.

Ethical Concerns with AI in Digital Spaces:

The use of AI in social connection raises ethical concerns that must be carefully addressed.

- **Bias and Discrimination:** AI algorithms can perpetuate existing biases, leading to discriminatory outcomes. Ensure that your AI tools are trained on diverse datasets and regularly audited for bias.
- **Privacy and Data Security:** AI systems collect and analyze vast amounts of user data. Implement robust data privacy and security measures to protect user information.
- **Transparency and Explainability:** The decision-making processes of AI algorithms can be opaque. Strive for transparency and explainability in your AI systems.
- **Job Displacement:** The automation of tasks through AI can lead to job displacement in certain sectors. Consider the potential impact of AI on employment and invest in retraining and upskilling programs.

By understanding the applications, benefits, and potential challenges of AI, you can leverage its power to enhance social connection, personalize user experiences, and optimize your online strategies. However, it is crucial to address the ethical concerns surrounding AI and ensure that its use aligns with your values and promotes a positive and inclusive digital environment. Continuous monitoring, evaluation, and adaptation are essential for navigating the evolving landscape of AI in social connection.

Chapter 4: Mastering Digital Communication

Effective communication is the cornerstone of building strong relationships, fostering engagement, and achieving your goals in the digital realm. This chapter explores the nuances of digital communication, providing practical strategies for conveying your message clearly, connecting with your audience authentically, and navigating the complexities of online interaction. We'll cover effective communication techniques, the art of persuasion in digital spaces, tailoring messages for different platforms, understanding nonverbal communication in digital interactions, overcoming language barriers, and improving response time and engagement.

Effective Communication Techniques Online:

Digital communication requires a nuanced approach, adapting traditional communication principles to the unique characteristics of the online environment.

- **Clarity and Conciseness:** Online audiences have short attention spans. Communicate your message clearly and concisely, using simple language and avoiding jargon. Get to the point quickly and use visuals to enhance understanding.
- **Active Listening:** Even in written communication, active listening is crucial. Pay attention to the nuances of language, ask clarifying questions, and respond thoughtfully to comments and messages.
- **Empathy and Emotional Intelligence:** Demonstrate empathy and understanding in your online interactions. Acknowledge others' feelings and perspectives, even when you disagree.
- **Positive Language:** Frame your messages positively and avoid negativity or criticism. Focus on solutions and opportunities.

The Art of Persuasion in Digital Spaces:

Persuasion in the digital age involves crafting compelling narratives, building trust, and appealing to your audience's emotions and values.

- **Storytelling:** Use storytelling to connect with your audience on an emotional level. Craft narratives that resonate with their experiences and aspirations.
- **Building Credibility:** Establish your expertise and build trust by providing valuable content, sharing your credentials, and engaging authentically.
- **Appealing to Emotions:** Connect with your audience's emotions by using evocative language, compelling visuals, and relatable stories.
- **Call to Action:** Clearly state the desired action you want your audience to take, whether it's visiting your website, making a purchase, or signing up for your newsletter.

Tailoring Messages for Different Platforms:

Each digital platform has its own unique culture and communication style. Tailor your messages to the specific platform you're using to maximize their impact.

- **Formal vs. Informal:** LinkedIn requires a more formal tone than platforms like Twitter or Instagram.
- **Visual vs. Text-Based:** Instagram and TikTok are visually driven platforms, while Twitter and Facebook rely more on text-based communication.
- **Character Limits:** Twitter imposes character limits, requiring concise messaging.
- **Hashtags:** Use relevant hashtags on platforms like Twitter and Instagram to increase discoverability.

Nonverbal Communication in Digital Interactions:

While nonverbal cues like body language and facial expressions are absent in online communication, other forms of nonverbal communication play a crucial role.

- **Emojis and Emoticons:** Use emojis and emoticons judiciously to convey emotions and tone.
- **Typography and Formatting:** Use bolding, italics, and other formatting techniques to emphasize key points.
- **Visuals:** Images, GIFs, and videos can convey emotions and enhance your message.

Overcoming Language Barriers Online:

In the global digital landscape, language barriers can hinder effective communication. Utilize translation tools and be mindful of cultural nuances.

- **Translation Tools:** Use translation tools to communicate with audiences who speak different languages. However, be aware that machine translation is not always perfect and can sometimes lead to misinterpretations.
- **Cultural Sensitivity:** Be mindful of cultural differences in communication styles and avoid using slang or idioms that may not be universally understood.

Improving Response Time and Engagement:

Responding promptly to comments, messages, and inquiries demonstrates respect for your audience and fosters engagement.

- **Set aside dedicated time for engagement:** Allocate specific times each day or week to respond to comments, messages, and inquiries.

- **Use social media management tools:** Social media management tools can help you streamline your engagement efforts and track conversations.
- **Prioritize timely responses:** Aim to respond to inquiries within 24 hours or as soon as reasonably possible.

By mastering the art of digital communication, you can build stronger relationships, foster engagement, and achieve your goals in the online world. Remember that effective communication is a two-way street. Listen actively, empathize with your audience, and adapt your communication style to the specific platform and context. Continuously refining your communication skills and staying attuned to the evolving digital landscape are crucial for success.

Chapter 5: Building Digital Leadership

In the interconnected digital world, leadership extends beyond traditional boundaries, encompassing online communities, social movements, and virtual collaborations. This chapter explores the principles and practices of effective digital leadership, empowering individuals to inspire, influence, and mobilize communities in the online space. We'll delve into leading communities and online movements, influencing change through digital leadership, the role of mentorship in online spaces, the art of public speaking and webinars in a digital context, writing and publishing thought leadership content, and building a leadership brand online.

Leading Communities and Online Movements:

Digital leaders cultivate thriving online communities by fostering a sense of belonging, shared purpose, and collective action. They empower members, facilitate collaboration, and inspire positive change.

- **Building Community:** Create a welcoming and inclusive environment where members feel comfortable sharing their thoughts, ideas, and experiences. Establish clear community guidelines and moderate discussions effectively.
- **Shared Vision:** Articulate a clear and inspiring vision for the community. Define shared goals and objectives that unite members and motivate collective action.
- **Empowering Members:** Empower community members to take ownership and contribute their unique talents and perspectives. Delegate responsibilities and provide opportunities for leadership development.

Influencing Change Through Digital Leadership:

Digital platforms offer powerful tools for advocating for change, raising awareness about important issues, and mobilizing collective action. Effective digital leaders leverage these platforms to inspire positive change in the world.

- **Advocacy and Awareness:** Use your digital platform to raise awareness about social issues, advocate for policy changes, and mobilize support for important causes.
- **Building Coalitions:** Collaborate with other individuals, organizations, and communities to amplify your message and achieve shared goals.
- **Mobilizing Action:** Encourage your audience to take concrete actions, such as signing petitions, contacting elected officials, or donating to charitable organizations.

The Role of Mentorship in Online Spaces:

Mentorship plays a crucial role in developing future leaders and empowering individuals to reach their full potential. Digital platforms provide accessible and scalable avenues for mentorship.

- **Online Mentoring Programs:** Create or participate in online mentoring programs that connect experienced professionals with aspiring leaders.
- **Virtual Mentorship Sessions:** Utilize video conferencing and other online tools to conduct virtual mentorship sessions.
- **Building Mentorship Networks:** Connect mentors and mentees through online platforms and communities.

Public Speaking and Webinars in a Digital Context:

Public speaking and webinars offer opportunities to share your expertise, connect with your audience, and build your leadership brand. Adapt your presentation style to the digital format and leverage interactive features to engage your audience.

- **Engaging Virtual Presentations:** Create visually appealing presentations that capture attention and convey information effectively. Use storytelling, humor, and other engagement techniques to keep your audience interested.
- **Interactive Webinars:** Incorporate interactive elements, such as polls, Q&A sessions, and live chat, to engage your audience and foster participation.
- **Platform Proficiency:** Familiarize yourself with the features and functionalities of different webinar platforms to ensure a smooth and professional presentation.

Writing and Publishing Thought Leadership Content:

Sharing your insights and perspectives through thought leadership content can establish you as a credible voice in your field and enhance your leadership brand.

- **Develop a Content Strategy:** Define your target audience, identify key topics, and create a content calendar to ensure consistent publishing.
- **High-Quality Content:** Create well-researched, insightful, and engaging content that provides value to your audience.
- **Guest Blogging and Publications:** Contribute articles to industry publications and guest blog on relevant websites to reach a wider audience.

Building a Leadership Brand Online:

Building a strong leadership brand online requires consistent effort, authentic engagement, and a clear articulation of your values and vision.

- **Define Your Leadership Brand:** What are your core values? What is your leadership style? What message do you want to convey to the world?
- **Consistent Online Presence:** Maintain a consistent presence across your digital platforms, using a professional profile picture, bio, and messaging.
- **Engage with Your Audience:** Respond to comments and messages, participate in discussions, and build relationships with your followers.
- **Showcase Your Expertise:** Share your knowledge, insights, and accomplishments to demonstrate your expertise and build credibility.

By actively leading online communities, influencing positive change, mentoring aspiring leaders, mastering the art of digital public speaking, publishing thought leadership content, and building a strong leadership brand, you can become a powerful force for good in the digital world. Remember that digital leadership is an ongoing journey of learning, growth, and adaptation. Continuously refine your skills, embrace new technologies, and stay connected with your audience to build a lasting and impactful leadership presence online.

Chapter 6: Managing Digital Wellbeing

The digital age offers unprecedented opportunities for connection, learning, and entertainment, but it also presents challenges to our mental and emotional wellbeing. This chapter explores the importance of maintaining a healthy relationship with technology, establishing boundaries, and prioritizing self-care in the digital realm. We'll delve into the concepts of digital detox and mental health, setting healthy boundaries online, avoiding digital overload, understanding the impact of social media on self-esteem, utilizing tools for digital mindfulness, and creating a balanced digital life.

Digital Detox and Mental Health:

The constant connectivity of the digital age can lead to stress, anxiety, and feelings of overwhelm. Taking regular breaks from technology through digital detoxes can improve mental health, reduce stress, and enhance focus and productivity.

- **Scheduled Digital Detoxes:** Set aside specific times each day or week to disconnect from technology. This could involve turning off notifications, putting away your phone, or engaging in activities that don't involve screens.
- **Mindful Technology Use:** Be intentional about your technology use. Avoid mindlessly scrolling through social media or checking your email constantly. Set limits on your screen time and be mindful of the impact of technology on your mental state.
- **Recognizing Signs of Digital Overload:** Be aware of the signs of digital overload, such as difficulty concentrating, irritability, sleep disturbances, and feelings of anxiety.

Setting Healthy Boundaries Online:

Establishing clear boundaries around your technology use is crucial for maintaining a healthy work-life balance and protecting your mental wellbeing.

- **Time Limits:** Set limits on the amount of time you spend on social media, email, and other online activities. Use apps or browser extensions to track your screen time and enforce limits.
- **Notification Management:** Turn off non-essential notifications to minimize distractions and reduce the urge to constantly check your phone.
- **Email Management:** Set specific times for checking and responding to emails. Avoid constantly checking your inbox throughout the day.
- **Social Media Boundaries:** Be mindful of the time you spend on social media. Unfollow accounts that trigger negative emotions or comparison. Curate your feed to prioritize positive and uplifting content.

Avoiding Digital Overload:

Digital overload can lead to feelings of stress, anxiety, and overwhelm. Managing your digital consumption and prioritizing offline activities is crucial for preventing burnout.

- **Mindful Consumption:** Be selective about the information you consume online. Avoid excessive exposure to negative news or social media drama.
- **Prioritizing Offline Activities:** Make time for activities that don't involve screens, such as spending time in nature, exercising, reading, or socializing with friends and family.
- **Time Management Techniques:** Implement time management techniques, such as the Pomodoro

Technique, to improve focus and productivity and reduce the temptation to multitask with digital devices.

The Impact of Social Media on Self-Esteem:

Social media can have a significant impact on self-esteem, particularly for young people. The curated nature of online profiles can lead to social comparison, feelings of inadequacy, and body image issues.

- **Critical Consumption of Social Media:** Encourage critical consumption of social media. Remind yourself that online profiles often present an idealized version of reality.
- **Focusing on Real-Life Connections:** Prioritize real-life connections and relationships over online interactions.
- **Seeking Support:** If you are struggling with the impact of social media on your self-esteem, seek support from a therapist or counselor.

Tools for Digital Mindfulness:

Various tools and techniques can promote digital mindfulness and help you develop a healthier relationship with technology.

- **Mindfulness Apps:** Mindfulness apps offer guided meditations and exercises that can help you cultivate present moment awareness and reduce stress.
- **Digital Wellbeing Features:** Many smartphones and operating systems now offer built-in digital wellbeing features, such as screen time tracking and app limits.
- **Website Blockers:** Website blockers can help you limit your access to distracting websites and apps.

Creating a Balanced Digital Life:

Balancing your online and offline activities is crucial for maintaining a healthy and fulfilling life. Integrate technology mindfully into your daily routine, prioritize real-life connections, and make time for activities that nourish your mind, body, and soul.

- **Setting Priorities:** Identify your priorities and values. Make sure your technology use aligns with your goals and values.
- **Time Management:** Manage your time effectively to ensure that you have time for both online and offline activities.
- **Self-Care:** Prioritize self-care activities, such as exercise, healthy eating, and quality sleep.

By understanding the potential impact of technology on your wellbeing, setting healthy boundaries, practicing digital mindfulness, and prioritizing self-care, you can create a balanced and fulfilling digital life that enhances your overall wellbeing. Remember that managing your digital wellbeing is an ongoing process. Continuously evaluate your relationship with technology, adapt your habits as needed, and prioritize your mental and emotional health.

Part 6:

The Future of Digital Social Connections

Chapter 1: Trends Shaping the Future of Social Media

The digital landscape is in constant flux, with new technologies and platforms emerging at a rapid pace. Understanding the trends shaping the future of social media is crucial for staying ahead of the curve, adapting your strategies, and maximizing your impact in the ever-evolving online world. This chapter explores the key trends that are poised to transform social media in the coming years, including emerging social media platforms, the rise of virtual and augmented reality, the impact of 5G on digital interactions, the evolving role of social media in the metaverse, the increasing importance of artificial intelligence, and the growing emphasis on user privacy and data security.

Emerging Social Media Platforms:

The social media landscape is constantly evolving, with new platforms emerging and existing platforms adapting to changing user preferences. Staying informed about these emerging platforms and their unique features is crucial for reaching new audiences and diversifying your online presence.

- **Niche Platforms:** Niche social media platforms catering to specific interests, communities, or demographics are gaining popularity. These platforms offer a more focused and engaged audience, providing opportunities for targeted marketing and community building.
- **Decentralized Social Media:** Decentralized platforms, built on blockchain technology, offer greater user control over data and privacy. These platforms are still in their early stages of development but have the

potential to disrupt the traditional social media landscape.

- **Audio-Based Social Media:** The rise of audio-based social media, such as Clubhouse and Twitter Spaces, offers new opportunities for real-time conversations, discussions, and community building.

The Rise of Virtual and Augmented Reality (VR/AR):

Virtual reality (VR) and augmented reality (AR) are poised to transform social media, creating immersive and interactive experiences that blur the lines between the physical and digital worlds.

- **VR Social Platforms:** VR social platforms allow users to interact in virtual environments, creating new possibilities for social connection, gaming, and entertainment.
- **AR Filters and Lenses:** AR filters and lenses are becoming increasingly popular on social media, enhancing user-generated content and providing opportunities for brands to engage with their audience in creative ways.
- **Immersive Brand Experiences:** VR and AR offer brands new opportunities to create immersive and interactive brand experiences, such as virtual product demonstrations or interactive games.

The Impact of 5G on Digital Interactions:

The rollout of 5G technology promises faster internet speeds, lower latency, and increased bandwidth, which will significantly impact social media and online interactions.

- **Enhanced Live Streaming:** 5G will enable higher quality live streams with reduced buffering and improved interactivity.
- **Real-Time Interactions:** Lower latency will facilitate more seamless and real-time interactions, such as video calls and online gaming.
- **Augmented Reality Experiences:** 5G will enable more complex and sophisticated AR experiences, enhancing social media filters, lenses, and interactive games.

Social Media and the Metaverse:

The metaverse, a persistent and immersive virtual world, is rapidly evolving, and social media is expected to play a central role in its development.

- **Virtual Communities:** The metaverse will host virtual communities where users can interact, socialize, and build relationships.
- **Virtual Events and Experiences:** Brands and creators will host virtual events, concerts, and other experiences in the metaverse, accessible through social media platforms.
- **Digital Avatars and Identities:** Users will create digital avatars to represent themselves in the metaverse, expressing their individuality and connecting with others in new ways.

The Increasing Importance of Artificial Intelligence (AI):

AI is playing an increasingly important role in shaping the social media landscape, powering personalized recommendations, content moderation, and targeted advertising.

- **Personalized Content Feeds:** AI algorithms curate personalized content feeds based on user preferences and behavior.
- **AI-Powered Content Moderation:** AI tools are used to detect and remove harmful content, such as hate speech and misinformation.
- **Targeted Advertising:** AI powers targeted advertising campaigns, ensuring that ads are seen by the most relevant audiences.

User Privacy and Data Security:

As users become increasingly concerned about data privacy and security, social media platforms are facing growing pressure to protect user information.

- **Data Privacy Regulations:** Governments around the world are implementing stricter data privacy regulations, such as GDPR and CCPA.
- **Increased Transparency:** Social media platforms are being asked to be more transparent about their data collection and usage practices.
- **User Control Over Data:** Users are demanding greater control over their personal data, including the ability to access, modify, and delete their data.

By understanding these emerging trends, social media users, businesses, and creators can adapt their strategies, embrace new technologies, and position themselves for success in the evolving digital landscape. Continuous learning, experimentation, and a willingness to adapt are crucial for navigating the exciting future of social media.

Chapter 2: Envisioning the Future of Social Media: A Hypothetical Scenario

While predicting the future with certainty is impossible, we can explore potential scenarios based on current trends and emerging technologies. This chapter presents a hypothetical vision of what social media might look like in the coming years, extrapolating from the trends discussed in the previous chapter. This is not a definitive prediction, but rather a thought experiment exploring the possibilities and potential implications of these evolving technologies.

The Immersive Metaverse as a Social Hub:

Imagine a world where social interaction primarily takes place in a persistent, interconnected metaverse. Instead of scrolling through feeds on a flat screen, users don their VR headsets and step into vibrant virtual environments where they interact with friends, family, and colleagues as personalized avatars. These avatars, meticulously crafted to reflect individual styles and personalities, become our primary digital identities. Social media platforms evolve into portals to this metaverse, offering seamless integration between the physical and digital worlds.

- **Personalized Virtual Worlds:** Users customize their virtual homes and environments, showcasing their interests and creating personalized spaces for social gatherings. Imagine hosting a virtual birthday party in your custom-designed metaverse mansion, inviting friends from across the globe to join the celebration.
- **Enhanced Social Interaction:** Advanced haptic suits and sensory technologies add a tactile dimension to virtual interactions, allowing users to experience virtual hugs, handshakes, and even the sensation of touch.

Imagine feeling the warmth of a virtual hug from a loved one who lives thousands of miles away.

- **Integrated Experiences:** Social media integrates seamlessly with other aspects of life, from shopping and entertainment to education and work. Imagine attending a virtual concert with friends, browsing virtual stores together, or collaborating on a project in a shared virtual workspace.

AI-Powered Personalization and Content Creation:

Artificial intelligence becomes deeply interwoven into the fabric of social media, powering hyper-personalized experiences and automating content creation.

- **AI-Curated Content:** AI algorithms curate personalized content feeds tailored to individual interests and preferences, eliminating information overload and maximizing engagement. Imagine a social media feed that anticipates your needs and delivers precisely the content you want to see, when you want to see it.
- **AI-Generated Content:** Users collaborate with AI tools to create personalized content, from stylized avatars and virtual environments to AI-generated music and art. Imagine co-creating a music video with an AI, customizing the visuals, music, and choreography to your liking.
- **AI-Powered Assistants:** Virtual assistants manage our social media presence, scheduling posts, responding to messages, and even generating content on our behalf, freeing up our time and maximizing efficiency.

The Rise of Decentralized and Privacy-Focused Platforms:

Concerns about data privacy and the centralized control of large social media companies fuel the growth of decentralized social networks built on blockchain technology.

- **User-Owned Data:** Users regain control of their data, choosing what information to share and with whom. Imagine a social media platform where you own your data and can monetize it directly, cutting out the intermediaries.
- **Enhanced Privacy and Security:** Blockchain technology enhances privacy and security, making it more difficult for data to be compromised or misused.
- **Community-Owned Platforms:** Decentralized governance models empower communities to manage and control their own social platforms, fostering greater transparency and accountability.

The Evolution of Influencer Marketing:

Influencer marketing evolves to embrace authenticity and transparency, with a greater emphasis on building genuine connections with audiences.

- **Micro-Influencers and Niche Communities:** Micro-influencers with smaller, highly engaged audiences gain prominence, offering brands more targeted and authentic reach.
- **Transparency and Authenticity:** Stricter regulations and increased user awareness demand greater transparency in sponsored content and influencer marketing campaigns. Authenticity becomes a key differentiator.
- **Virtual Influencers:** AI-powered virtual influencers gain popularity, offering brands greater control over their messaging and image.

The Blurring of Physical and Digital Realities:

The lines between the physical and digital worlds blur further, with augmented reality seamlessly integrating digital information and experiences into our physical surroundings.

- **AR Overlays and Interactive Experiences:** Social media platforms integrate AR overlays, providing real-time information about the world around us, from product reviews and historical facts to directions and social connections. Imagine pointing your phone at a restaurant and seeing reviews, menus, and even virtual avatars of friends who have dined there.
- **AR-Enhanced Social Interactions:** AR filters and lenses enhance face-to-face interactions, providing real-time information about the people we meet, their interests, and social connections.

This hypothetical scenario offers a glimpse into the potential future of social media, driven by emerging technologies and evolving user behaviors. While the exact trajectory of social media's evolution remains uncertain, one thing is clear: the future of social connection will be increasingly immersive, personalized, and interconnected. Adaptability, creativity, and a willingness to embrace new technologies will be essential for navigating this exciting new frontier.

Chapter 3: Social Media and the Metaverse: A Converging Future?

The metaverse, a persistent, shared, and immersive digital environment, holds the potential to revolutionize how we interact, connect, and experience the world. Social media, already a central part of our digital lives, is poised to play a crucial role in shaping the metaverse and how we engage with it. This chapter explores the potential convergence of social media and the metaverse, examining the opportunities and challenges this integration presents.

Social Media as the Gateway to the Metaverse:

Imagine accessing the metaverse not through a separate app or platform, but through your existing social media accounts. Your social connections, profile information, and even your digital assets could seamlessly transition into the metaverse, creating a unified and personalized experience. Social media platforms could evolve into portals to the metaverse, offering a familiar and intuitive interface for navigating this new digital frontier.

- **Unified Digital Identity:** Your social media profile could become the foundation for your metaverse identity, allowing you to maintain a consistent persona across both platforms. Imagine your carefully curated Instagram profile seamlessly translating into your metaverse avatar and virtual home.
- **Seamless Social Connections:** Your existing social connections could be ported into the metaverse, allowing you to easily connect with friends, family, and colleagues in virtual environments. Imagine attending a virtual concert with your Facebook friends or collaborating on a project with your LinkedIn network in a shared virtual workspace.

- **Cross-Platform Integration:** Social media platforms could integrate with various metaverse experiences, allowing you to share your virtual adventures, creations, and interactions with your existing social networks. Imagine posting a 360° photo of your virtual skydiving experience on Instagram or sharing a virtual trophy you earned in a metaverse game on Facebook.

The Evolution of Social Interaction in the Metaverse:

The metaverse promises to transform social interaction, offering new ways to connect, communicate, and build relationships. Social media platforms could play a key role in facilitating these interactions, providing tools and features for communication, collaboration, and community building.

- **Virtual Events and Gatherings:** Social media platforms could host virtual events and gatherings within the metaverse, bringing together people from around the world to share experiences and connect in new ways. Imagine attending a virtual music festival with friends or participating in a virtual conference with colleagues, all within the metaverse accessed through your social media account.
- **Enhanced Social Commerce:** Social media's role in e-commerce could expand within the metaverse, offering immersive shopping experiences and virtual marketplaces. Imagine browsing a virtual store with friends, trying on clothes with your avatar, and purchasing digital items that can be used both in the metaverse and in augmented reality experiences in the physical world.
- **Collaborative Creation:** Social media could facilitate collaborative creation within the metaverse, empowering users to build, design, and share virtual experiences together. Imagine collaborating with friends

on designing a virtual art installation or building a virtual community center within the metaverse.

Challenges and Considerations:

The integration of social media and the metaverse also presents significant challenges that need to be addressed.

- **Interoperability:** Ensuring seamless interoperability between different metaverse platforms and social media networks will be crucial for a unified and user-friendly experience.
- **Privacy and Data Security:** Protecting user data and privacy in the metaverse will be paramount. Robust security measures and transparent data policies will be essential.
- **Accessibility and Inclusivity:** The metaverse should be accessible to everyone, regardless of their physical abilities, socioeconomic status, or geographic location.
- **Governance and Moderation:** Establishing clear guidelines and effective moderation strategies will be crucial for maintaining a safe and positive environment within the metaverse.
- **Digital Identity and Ownership:** Defining digital identity and ownership within the metaverse will be complex. Questions around intellectual property, virtual asset ownership, and the authenticity of digital identities will need to be addressed.

The Future of Content Creation and Consumption:

The convergence of social media and the metaverse could revolutionize how we create and consume content.

- **Immersive Storytelling:** Creators could leverage the immersive environment of the metaverse to tell stories in new and engaging ways. Imagine experiencing a news story from within the event itself or exploring a historical period through a virtual recreation.

- **User-Generated Content:** User-generated content will likely play a significant role in shaping the metaverse. Users could create and share their own virtual experiences, games, and environments, contributing to the ever-evolving digital landscape.

- **Interactive and Gamified Content:** Social media content could become more interactive and gamified within the metaverse, offering users new ways to engage with brands and creators. Imagine participating in a virtual scavenger hunt organized by your favorite brand or playing a game to earn virtual rewards.

The convergence of social media and the metaverse presents both exciting opportunities and significant challenges. By addressing these challenges proactively and focusing on creating user-centric experiences, we can unlock the full potential of this evolving digital landscape and shape a future where social connection is more immersive, engaging, and meaningful than ever before. This is a future still being written, and its ultimate shape will depend on the choices we make today.

Chapter 4: The Future of Digital Connections: A Hypothetical Exploration

The way we connect, communicate, and build relationships online is constantly evolving. Extrapolating from current trends, we can envision a future where digital connections become even more integrated into our lives, blurring the lines between the physical and digital worlds and offering new possibilities for human interaction. This chapter explores a potential future for digital connections, considering the potential impact of emerging technologies, evolving social behaviors, and the ongoing quest for more meaningful online experiences.

Hyper-Personalization and AI-Driven Connections:

Imagine a future where artificial intelligence plays a central role in shaping our digital connections. AI algorithms could analyze our online behavior, preferences, and social interactions to curate personalized experiences and connect us with like-minded individuals.

- **AI-Powered Matchmaking:** Social platforms could use AI to connect us with people who share our interests, values, and goals, facilitating deeper and more meaningful connections. Imagine a social network that goes beyond surface-level connections and matches you with individuals who share your passions and aspirations.
- **Personalized Content and Recommendations:** AI algorithms could curate personalized content feeds, filtering out noise and delivering information and entertainment tailored to our individual preferences. Imagine a world where you never have to scroll through

endless irrelevant content, as your digital feeds are perfectly curated to your tastes.

- **AI-Enhanced Communication:** AI-powered translation tools could break down language barriers, facilitating seamless communication between people from different cultures and backgrounds. Imagine a world where language is no longer a barrier to connection and collaboration.

The Rise of Immersive and Sensory Experiences:

Emerging technologies like virtual reality (VR), augmented reality (AR), and haptic feedback could transform digital connections into multi-sensory experiences, blurring the lines between the physical and digital worlds.

- **Virtual Shared Experiences:** VR and AR could enable us to share immersive experiences with others, regardless of our physical location. Imagine attending a virtual concert with friends from across the globe or exploring a virtual museum together.
- **Haptic Communication:** Haptic feedback technology could add a tactile dimension to digital communication, allowing us to experience the sensation of touch in virtual interactions. Imagine feeling a virtual hug from a loved one who lives far away or shaking hands with a new business contact in a virtual meeting.
- **Augmented Social Interactions:** AR overlays could enhance our real-world interactions, providing real-time information about the people we meet and the places we visit. Imagine looking at someone through your AR glasses and seeing their social media profile, interests, and shared connections.

The Evolution of Digital Communities:

Online communities could evolve into vibrant, self-governing ecosystems, powered by blockchain technology and decentralized governance models.

- **Decentralized Social Networks:** Blockchain-based social networks could empower users with greater control over their data and privacy, fostering greater trust and transparency. Imagine a social network that is owned and governed by its users, not a centralized corporation.
- **Tokenized Communities:** Community tokens could incentivize participation and reward valuable contributions, creating a more equitable and sustainable ecosystem. Imagine earning tokens for contributing valuable content or participating in community events.
- **DAO-Governed Communities:** Decentralized Autonomous Organizations (DAOs) could enable communities to govern themselves democratically, making decisions collectively and shaping the future of their digital spaces.

The Quest for Meaningful Connection:

As the digital world becomes increasingly saturated with information and superficial interactions, the quest for meaningful connection will become even more important.

- **Focus on Quality over Quantity:** Users may prioritize smaller, more intimate online communities and connections over large, impersonal networks. Imagine focusing your online energy on a few close-knit communities rather than trying to maintain a vast network of superficial connections.

- **Authenticity and Transparency:** Authenticity and transparency will become increasingly valued in online interactions, as users seek genuine connections and meaningful relationships.
- **Digital Wellbeing and Mindfulness:** As we become more aware of the potential downsides of excessive technology use, digital wellbeing and mindfulness practices will become increasingly important. Imagine integrating digital detox rituals and mindfulness techniques into your daily routine to maintain a healthy relationship with technology.

The Ethical Considerations of Advanced Digital Connections:

The increasing integration of AI and immersive technologies into our digital connections raises ethical considerations that must be addressed.

- **AI Bias and Fairness:** Ensuring that AI algorithms are fair and unbiased will be crucial for preventing discrimination and promoting inclusivity in digital spaces.
- **Data Privacy and Security:** Protecting user data and privacy in the metaverse and other immersive environments will be paramount.
- **Digital Identity and Authenticity:** Establishing secure and verifiable digital identities will be essential for building trust and preventing fraud in the metaverse.
- **Accessibility and Inclusivity:** Ensuring that these advanced digital connection tools and platforms are accessible to everyone, regardless of their physical abilities or socioeconomic status, will be crucial for promoting equity and inclusion.

The future of digital connections holds immense potential for enhancing human interaction, fostering deeper relationships, and creating more meaningful online experiences. However, realizing this potential requires careful consideration of the ethical implications and a commitment to building a future where technology serves humanity's best interests. This future is not predetermined; it is being shaped by the choices we make today.

Chapter 5: The Future of Digital Communities: A Hypothetical Exploration

Digital communities have become integral to our lives, offering spaces for connection, collaboration, and shared interests. As technology continues to evolve, these communities are poised for transformation, potentially leading to more immersive, personalized, and decentralized experiences. This chapter explores a hypothetical vision of the future of digital communities, considering the potential impact of emerging technologies, shifting social dynamics, and the ongoing quest for deeper connection in the digital age.

Immersive and Interactive Communities in the Metaverse:

Imagine digital communities existing not just as forums or social media groups, but as vibrant, three-dimensional spaces within the metaverse. Users, represented by personalized avatars, could interact in real-time, fostering a sense of presence and shared experience that transcends geographical limitations.

- **Virtual Community Spaces:** Communities could build and customize their own virtual spaces within the metaverse, reflecting their shared identity and interests. Imagine a virtual book club meeting in a cozy, book-lined virtual room or a virtual gaming community gathering in a futuristic virtual arena.
- **Enhanced Social Interaction:** Advanced avatar technology and haptic feedback could enable more nuanced and expressive communication, blurring the lines between physical and digital interaction. Imagine sharing a virtual high-five with a teammate after a collaborative project or experiencing the warmth of a virtual hug from a friend.

- **Shared Experiences and Events:** Communities could host virtual events, workshops, and gatherings, fostering deeper connections and shared experiences among members. Imagine attending a virtual cooking class with fellow foodies or participating in a virtual yoga retreat with your online wellness community.

AI-Powered Community Management and Personalization:

Artificial intelligence could play an increasingly important role in managing and shaping digital communities, automating tasks, personalizing experiences, and fostering deeper connections.

- **AI-Powered Moderation:** AI algorithms could assist with community moderation, identifying and filtering harmful content, and promoting positive interactions. Imagine a community free from spam, harassment, and negativity, thanks to intelligent moderation tools.
- **Personalized Community Experiences:** AI could analyze user data to personalize community experiences, recommending relevant content, connecting members with shared interests, and tailoring the community environment to individual preferences. Imagine joining a community and instantly feeling welcomed and connected, with AI-powered recommendations guiding you to relevant discussions and resources.
- **AI-Facilitated Collaboration:** AI tools could facilitate collaboration within communities, automating tasks, coordinating projects, and connecting members with complementary skills and expertise. Imagine collaborating on a community project with AI assistance, streamlining communication, and optimizing workflow.

Decentralized and Autonomous Communities:

Blockchain technology and decentralized autonomous organizations (DAOs) could empower communities with greater control over their governance, finances, and future direction.

- **DAO-Governed Communities:** Members could collectively make decisions about community rules, resource allocation, and future development through democratic voting mechanisms. Imagine a community where every member has a voice and a stake in its future.
- **Tokenized Incentives and Rewards:** Community tokens could incentivize participation, reward valuable contributions, and create a more sustainable economic model for digital communities. Imagine earning tokens for contributing helpful content, organizing community events, or mentoring new members.
- **Enhanced Transparency and Trust:** Blockchain technology could enhance transparency and accountability within communities, providing a secure and immutable record of all transactions and decisions.

The Evolution of Community Identity and Belonging:

As digital communities become more immersive and personalized, the sense of community identity and belonging could deepen, blurring the lines between online and offline relationships.

- **Hybrid Online/Offline Communities:** Digital communities could extend beyond the virtual world, organizing real-world meetups, events, and activities to strengthen connections and foster a sense of community in the physical realm. Imagine attending a local meetup with members of your online writing group or participating in a charity run organized by your online fitness community.

- **Stronger Social Bonds:** The immersive and personalized nature of future digital communities could foster stronger social bonds and more meaningful relationships between members. Imagine forming deep friendships and connections with people you've only ever met in the metaverse.

Challenges and Opportunities:

The evolution of digital communities presents both exciting opportunities and significant challenges.

- **Addressing Inclusivity and Accessibility:** Ensuring that these future communities are inclusive and accessible to everyone, regardless of their technical skills, socioeconomic status, or geographic location, will be crucial.
- **Protecting User Privacy and Security:** Safeguarding user data and privacy in increasingly immersive and interconnected digital environments will require robust security measures and transparent data policies.
- **Navigating the Ethical Implications of AI:** As AI plays a larger role in community management and personalization, addressing potential biases and ensuring ethical use of these technologies will be essential.
- **Fostering Authentic Connection:** Maintaining authenticity and genuine connection in increasingly virtualized communities will be crucial for preventing alienation and fostering a sense of belonging.

The future of digital communities holds immense potential for fostering connection, collaboration, and shared growth. By embracing emerging technologies responsibly, prioritizing user needs, and addressing the ethical considerations of this evolving landscape, we can create digital communities that are more vibrant, inclusive, and meaningful than ever before. This future is not predetermined; it is being shaped by the choices we make today.

Chapter 6: The Future of Digital Connections and Society: A Hypothetical Exploration

The pervasive influence of digital technologies is reshaping not only how we connect with each other but also the very fabric of society. This chapter explores potential future scenarios for digital connections and their broader societal impact, considering the potential implications for education, work, healthcare, governance, and human relationships.

Transforming Education and Learning:

Imagine a future where education transcends the confines of traditional classrooms, leveraging immersive technologies and personalized learning platforms to create engaging and accessible learning experiences.

- **Personalized Learning in the Metaverse:** Students could learn in interactive virtual environments, tailored to their individual learning styles and pace. Imagine exploring ancient Rome in a virtual reality history class or dissecting a virtual frog in a biology lab.
- **AI-Powered Tutors and Mentors:** AI-powered tutors and mentors could provide personalized guidance and support, helping students master complex concepts and achieve their learning goals. Imagine having a virtual tutor available 24/7 to answer your questions and provide feedback.
- **Global Classrooms and Collaborative Learning:** Digital platforms could connect students from around the world, fostering cross-cultural understanding and collaborative learning opportunities. Imagine collaborating on a project with students from different countries, sharing diverse perspectives and learning from each other.

The Future of Work and Collaboration:

The nature of work is evolving rapidly, with remote work, flexible schedules, and digital collaboration becoming increasingly prevalent. The future of work could be even more decentralized, flexible, and interconnected.

- **Decentralized Autonomous Organizations (DAOs) and the Future of Work:** DAOs could revolutionize how we organize and manage work, enabling decentralized decision-making, transparent governance, and equitable distribution of rewards. Imagine working for a DAO where you have a say in company decisions and share in the profits.
- **Remote Collaboration in the Metaverse:** Virtual and augmented reality could transform remote collaboration, enabling colleagues to interact in shared virtual spaces, enhancing teamwork and communication. Imagine brainstorming with your team in a virtual office or collaborating on a design project in a shared virtual workspace.
- **AI-Powered Skill Development and Job Matching:** AI algorithms could analyze individual skills and match them with relevant job opportunities, facilitating career development and workforce mobility. Imagine a platform that automatically matches your skills and experience with open positions that align with your career goals.

Revolutionizing Healthcare with Digital Connections:

Digital technologies are already transforming healthcare, from telehealth consultations to remote patient monitoring. The future of healthcare could be even more personalized, accessible, and data-driven.

- **Telemedicine and Remote Patient Monitoring:** Advanced sensors and wearable devices could enable continuous remote monitoring of patients' health, providing real-time data to healthcare providers and enabling proactive interventions. Imagine receiving personalized health recommendations based on real-time data from your smartwatch.
- **AI-Powered Diagnostics and Treatment:** AI algorithms could analyze medical images, patient records, and genetic data to assist with diagnosis, personalize treatment plans, and accelerate drug discovery. Imagine receiving a faster and more accurate diagnosis thanks to AI-powered diagnostic tools.
- **Virtual Reality Therapy and Rehabilitation:** VR and AR could be used for therapeutic purposes, providing immersive experiences for treating phobias, anxiety disorders, and physical rehabilitation. Imagine overcoming your fear of heights through a VR therapy session or practicing physical therapy exercises in a virtual environment.

Reimagining Governance and Civic Engagement:

Digital platforms could empower citizens with greater access to information, facilitate participation in democratic processes, and promote transparency and accountability in governance.

- **E-Governance and Digital Voting:** Secure online voting platforms could increase voter turnout and make elections more accessible. Imagine voting securely from your smartphone or computer, eliminating the need to travel to a polling station.
- **Citizen Assemblies and Online Deliberation:** Digital platforms could facilitate citizen assemblies and online deliberation, enabling citizens to participate directly in

policymaking and shaping the future of their communities.

- **Transparency and Accountability Through Blockchain:** Blockchain technology could enhance transparency and accountability in government by providing a secure and immutable record of transactions and decisions.

The Evolution of Human Relationships:

Digital connections are reshaping human relationships, creating new possibilities for connection, intimacy, and community. The future of relationships could be even more fluid, diverse, and interconnected.

- **Hybrid Online/Offline Relationships:** The lines between online and offline relationships could blur further, with digital interactions complementing and enhancing real-world connections. Imagine meeting someone online and then deepening that connection through shared experiences in both the digital and physical worlds.
- **Diverse and Inclusive Communities:** Digital platforms could foster diverse and inclusive communities, connecting people from different backgrounds and creating spaces for shared understanding and mutual support.
- **The Ethics of Digital Intimacy:** As technology mediates more of our relationships, ethical considerations around digital intimacy, consent, and online safety will become increasingly important.

The future of digital connections and their impact on society is full of both promise and potential challenges. By embracing innovation responsibly, prioritizing ethical considerations, and fostering a human-centered approach to technology development, we can harness the power of digital connections to create a more equitable, connected, and fulfilling future for all. This future is not predetermined; it is being shaped by the choices we make today.

CONCLUSION

Navigating the ever-evolving digital landscape demands a multifaceted approach, blending strategic foresight, ethical considerations, and a willingness to adapt to the ceaseless tide of emerging technologies. Building a robust and impactful online presence is no longer a mere option, but a necessity in today's interconnected world. This journey begins with crafting a compelling personal brand that resonates with your target audience, communicating your unique value proposition authentically and consistently. Creating value-driven content, whether through insightful blog posts, engaging videos, or interactive experiences, lies at the heart of attracting and retaining an engaged audience. Active participation in digital communities, fostering genuine connections, and contributing meaningfully to online conversations are crucial for building a loyal following and establishing yourself as a respected voice within your niche. Measuring the impact of your digital endeavors through data analysis and performance tracking enables informed decision-making, allowing you to refine your strategies and optimize your efforts for maximum reach and engagement.

Beyond simply establishing a presence, fostering genuine connections and strengthening digital relationships require a deep understanding of human interaction in the digital age. Active listening, empathetic communication, and building trust are essential for cultivating meaningful relationships online. Managing online communities effectively demands a nuanced understanding of group dynamics, conflict resolution strategies, and the importance of fostering a positive and inclusive environment. As visual content becomes increasingly dominant, mastering the art of visual storytelling, designing compelling graphics, and creating engaging videos are vital for capturing attention and conveying your message effectively. Promoting your content strategically, leveraging both organic reach and paid advertising, is crucial for amplifying your message and reaching a wider audience. The power of storytelling, whether through personal anecdotes, brand narratives, or compelling case studies, cannot be overstated; it is the key to connecting with your audience on an emotional level and making your message memorable and impactful.

Monetizing your digital presence requires a careful balance between generating revenue and maintaining ethical integrity. Understanding the nuances of influencer marketing, navigating potential conflicts of interest, and prioritizing transparency and authenticity are crucial for building a sustainable and trustworthy online business. Creating and selling digital products, offering consulting or coaching services, and leveraging affiliate marketing are just some of the avenues available for monetizing your expertise and online presence. However, ethical considerations must always be at the forefront of these endeavors.

Looking towards the future, leveraging data analytics, navigating the complexities of digital algorithms, and harnessing the transformative power of artificial intelligence become paramount for staying ahead of the curve. Data-driven decision-making, informed by insightful analysis and performance tracking, enables you to optimize your strategies, personalize user experiences, and predict future trends. Understanding how social media algorithms function and adapting to their ever-evolving nature is crucial for maximizing your reach and visibility. Artificial intelligence offers a wealth of opportunities for automating tasks, generating content, and personalizing user experiences, but it also presents ethical considerations that must be carefully addressed. As the metaverse continues to evolve, understanding its potential implications for social interaction, commerce, and community building will be essential for navigating this new digital frontier.

Ultimately, prioritizing digital wellbeing, setting healthy boundaries, and fostering inclusive online communities are fundamental for creating a positive and sustainable digital future. Managing digital overload, mitigating the negative impacts of social media on mental health, and promoting diversity and accessibility are crucial for building a healthy and equitable online environment. The digital landscape is not a static destination but a dynamic and ever-evolving journey shaped by the interplay of human connection, technological innovation, and societal shifts. By embracing a mindful, ethical, and adaptable approach, we can navigate this complex terrain, harness its transformative power for positive change, and shape a digital future that reflects our shared values and aspirations. The story of digital connection is far from over; it is continuously being written, and each of us has the opportunity to contribute to its next chapter.

www.ingramcontent.com/pod-product-compliance
Lightning Source LLC
Chambersburg PA
CBHW061346250726
48657CB00004B/1361